GW00393451

FOREVER

FOREVER

SAMANTHA FOX

*with LEIF ERIKSSON and
MARTIN SVENSSON*

An Imprint of Hal Leonard LLC

Published in 2017 by Backbeat Books
An Imprint of Hal Leonard LLC
7777 West Bluemound Road
Milwaukee, WI 53213

Trade Book Division Editorial Offices
33 Plymouth St., Montclair, NJ 07042

All photos are from the author's collection, unless otherwise noted.

Printed in the United States of America
Book design by Kristina Rolander

Library of Congress Cataloging-in-Publication Data
Names: Fox, Samantha. | Eriksson, Leif, 1957- | Svensson, Martin, 1978-
Title: Forever / Samantha Fox with Leif Eriksson and Martin Svensson.
Description: Montclair, NJ : Backbeat Books, 2017.
Identifiers: LCCN 2017018628 | ISBN 9781617136900
Subjects: LCSH: Fox, Samantha. | Singers--England--Biography. | LCGFT:
  Autobiographies.
Classification: LCC ML420.F758 A3 2017 | DDC 782.42164092 [B] --dc23
LC record available at https://lccn.loc.gov/2017018628

www.backbeatbooks.com

*Dedicated in loving memory
to Myra Stratton*

CONTENTS

February 9, 2015

This is what I remember: I'm sitting in a dressing room. It's small, with just one window. On the other side of the door, I can hear the makeup artists, stylists, and studio girls running around. They're talking excitedly in a language I can't understand.

The air feels thick and difficult to breathe. If I could, I would leave. If I could, I would be with Myra. The uncertainty, not having any idea how long she has left. Not having any idea whether she'll be alive when I wake. I can't remember the last time I slept a whole night through. It feels like everything is a haze.

There's a knock at the door. A voice through the crack: "Five minutes."

I force myself up and pull on my leather jacket. Pause in front of the mirror.

From up onstage, I can make out the intro to the song that brought me here, even if everything began in a completely different way—over thirty years ago.

1

THE SEARCH IS ON FOR THE FACE AND SHAPE OF 1983

"You have the face of a child and the body of
a woman; you remind me of my wife."

"Sammy, look at this!"

It was a typical Sunday. Mum, Dad, Vanessa, and I had eaten a Sunday roast like always, and we were spread out on the sofa and armchairs in the living room when Mum spotted the newspaper ad. It was the twelfth of December, a date I'll never forget because it was also Mum and Dad's wedding anniversary. I'll never forget the headline, either: "The Face and Shape of 1983."

Mum excitedly told us that the first prize was a thousand pounds, a portfolio of pictures taken by a professional photographer, and an international modeling contract.

As a young girl, she had dreamed of being a model herself, but she'd never been able to afford the right clothes or the cost of producing a portfolio. So the fact that she thought I should give it a go wasn't all that unusual—and at that time I was always being told by many people that I should be a model, as I was attracting a lot of attention from the opposite sex. Even though I had no interest in either makeup or clothes—my dream was to be an actress or a musician—I liked competing and performing and had already taken part in a number of different talent shows.

We lived in North London at the time, in Mount Pleasant Villas, not far from Terri Christopher, who, according to Mum, owned loads of sexy underwear. How she knew that, I have no idea. But Terri also happened to own a professional camera, and Mum called her that same evening to ask her to bring it over, along with some nice underwear—and the very next day we got to work.

It was me, Mum, Nan, Vanessa, and Terri. I remember we were in my bedroom on the top floor and that I was standing in front of a wall covered in Laura Ashley wallpaper. I was wearing a white Victorian basque, white lace gloves, white suspenders and stockings, and a pair of white high-heeled shoes. We'd borrowed everything from Terri.

Nan turned on a bedside lamp to try to create the right kind of light, and she gave me instructions on how to pose. Terri took the pictures, and Vanessa, who was ten, was her assistant. I remember we were all really happy when we were done. There was just one problem: the roll of film in the camera was several years old, and when we took it in for processing it soon became clear that we didn't have a single picture. Luckily, Mum had taken one with her own Kodak Brownie camera (one of those long, narrow ones), and on the back of that photograph she wrote my name, my measurements, our address, and our phone number, and sent it off to the newspaper.

Nineteen eighty-two was the first year that the *Sunday People* had run its Face and Shape competition, so I didn't really know what to expect. I actually didn't give it much thought at all. I mean, I was sixteen at the time, and struggling flat out with my A-levels at school.

But one day in early January 1983, the phone rang. Mum answered. A man from the *Sunday People* told her that over twenty thousand pictures had been sent in to the competition and that I was one of the twenty finalists. He wanted to know if I would take part in a photo session with the others ahead of the last few weeks. This was way before reality shows became big business, but the idea was that, just like in the reality shows we have now, the public (i.e., the readers) could follow our progress over the last few weeks in the newspaper.

I remember Mum was really enthusiastic, especially when she found out it would be John Kelly taking the pictures. He was a famous glamour model photographer at the time, married to the legendary page three girl Vivien Neves, who was also the first woman to appear naked on the front page of the *Times* in 1971. *The Times* was, and is, one of England's most respected papers, so it was a pretty big deal when that picture was published. Anyway, Mum said that if John Kelly was taking the pictures, we could be sure they would be tasteful. And just a few weeks later, it was time to go to his studio. I can't remember exactly where it was, but I know it was Sunday and that it was windy, rainy, and cold outside.

Usually, Mum and I talked nonstop, but when we stepped through the door into John's studio we both went quiet. Not because we were especially nervous; we just felt so embarrassed and inferior. I mean, Prince Andrew's ex-girlfriend was there, plus a load of other models with Louis Vuitton bags, designer gear, and perfect hair. Some even had tiny lapdogs with them—and they were all over twenty. I, on the other hand, wasn't wearing any makeup, had my hair in a ponytail, and was wearing a tracksuit, even if I did have Terri's Victorian basque thing in a bag. I could feel their eyes on me, like they were thinking, "Who is this little girl? She's just a kid."

Luckily, John had arranged for a makeup artist to fix up me and the others in a nearby room. John would take pictures of each of us in his actual studio after that. We were each given a number. I think I was tenth in line, but John had only taken a few pictures when he came over to me and said, "Is it OK if you wait out there till I'm done with the others? I want to try taking some different pictures of you, too." He looked a bit like a rocker, with long hair and a beard. And just like a rocker, he was pretty shy and didn't really look me in the eye when he talked.

I remember the bubbling feeling in my stomach, in any case. I mean, it was like being at the bottom of the hierarchy one minute, only to feel special and chosen the next. John, who was apparently also on the *Sunday People* jury that picked the finalists, continued, "The pictures we received were almost all professional. That's why we noticed yours. The measurements on the back of the picture caught our eye, too, of course." John explained that they couldn't quite believe that I had such big breasts and still such narrow hips. Then he went back to his camera and called in the next girl.

I left the studio and stood out in the corridor with Mum, waiting. I have no idea how long we stood there for, but once we were the only ones left, John came back out to us. He looked me up and down.

"Are you ready?"

I nodded.

"Great, then let's go."

I followed him in and John took a few new pictures. I know it might sound strange, but standing there in front of the camera really did feel completely natural. It was like I somehow knew exactly what to do.

After we'd been doing that for a while, John looked at me with a really happy expression for the first time, and said, "You have the face of a child and the body of a woman; you remind me of my wife . . . I think you could be a fantastic glamour model and a top page three girl."

I didn't know what to say. In the end, I mumbled something about how I thought I was far too short to be a glamour model.

But John just shook his head and said that Viv (his wife) was also petite, and that it had hardly been a problem for her.

"Plus, your legs are long enough in relation to your upper body; it means you look taller on film," he added. Then he asked if it was OK if he took a few topless pictures. He called for Mum to come in.

"Sam's got a natural talent; she could be huge. It's not just her breasts. She has a pretty face, and I just love her personality. I think she could be a star."

I could see that Mum was about to burst with pride, and I had no doubts. Because, if I'm crass about it, what was waiting for me once school was over? Getting married and having kids? You only had to look around where I lived; there were plenty of people who had kids young. Plenty who were unemployed. Plenty who had tough, low-paying jobs. I'd talked about joining the police in the past, then realized I was far too short. This could be my chance. But first, I needed Dad's blessing.

John showed Mum to a phone on the wall in the studio, and the minute she got through to Dad I knew he wasn't anywhere near as keen. John could hear it, too, because he went over to Mum and asked to talk to him. He repeated to Dad what he had just told us. And coming from a top photographer like John, even Dad realized it wasn't just talk. Though maybe he wasn't entirely convinced, because he asked to talk to me, too.

"You totally sure about this, Sammy?" he said. "You're still very young." But then Mum took the receiver and told him the pictures would be classy and tasteful. John spoke to Dad again and reassured him that they wouldn't be published anywhere. He only wanted to take them to show the editors at the *Sunday People*, and Dad finally gave his blessing.

I went back to my position in front of the camera, and soon after that I'd taken off my top. John snapped a few pictures as he said to Mum, "I'd prefer to continue with Sam alone, because if you're here she might act differently. I want her to feel free."

Mum did as he asked and left the room. But the door to the studio had a small pane of glass in it, and I could see the expression on her face through it the entire time. The way she was living that moment, she was looking so proud.

At any rate, the whole thing was pretty undramatic. I mean, this was a time when most girls sunbathed topless, and like many other mothers and daughters across England, Mum and I had been

5

following the page three girls in the *Sun* for as long as I could remember. They were practically minor celebrities. Women checked out their underwear and makeup. I remember that Mum used to say, "Oh, she's very pretty" (especially when it was Viv Neves), or "Look at her hair," the way women talk about other women. The men focused on other things, of course.

After that, it was just a case of waiting until the next Sunday, when the finalists' pictures were published. Or, more accurately, until late on Saturday, January 22, when the Sunday papers were delivered to the news kiosks. On that particular Saturday night, I was hanging out with the son of one of Mum's friends. His name was John, too, and like usual at that age when we wanted to get away from the adults, we were down by the abandoned railway tracks near our house. We had good reason to stay away that evening, too: John had promised me my first joint.

I remember he had rolled it in advance and kept it among the other cigarettes in the box of Chesterfields in the pocket of his jeans. Once he was sure there was no one around, he lit the joint and handed it to me.

I took a deep drag and noticed that familiar woody scent as the smoke hung around us like a white cloud.

"You need to be careful," John said. "It hits you afterwards . . . It's a creeper."

I shrugged and took a few more tokes. Once I had smoked the entire joint, I said, "Nothing's happening; I feel the same."

John rolled another, and once we finished that we started walking back towards my house. While we were walking, I suddenly felt sick, and by the time we made it inside, into the living room, I thought I was going to faint. Right then, Mum and Dad came in through the front door and up the stairs. "Sammy!"

Dad held up a copy of the *Sunday People* in my face, and as though through a cloud I saw myself topless on the front page. I didn't know what to do. I mean, I'd smoked grass for the first time, and there were my tits on the front page of one of England's biggest papers, despite John Kelly promising he was only going to show them to the editors.

Inside the paper, there were pictures of each of the finalists, and beneath mine it said, "Still a schoolgirl, Samantha, who also appears on page one, is busy studying for her A-levels in the sixth form of school."

That was when the grass really started to kick in. Mum said, "Look at her face; she's white as a sheet! She's gone all funny."

I sat down on the sofa with a thud and felt completely paranoid. I was thinking about school, about how I would have to go back after practically everyone had seen my breasts. And right then, John got the giggles. He was standing away from us with his face in his hands, and as soon as he looked up he laughed so much that his eyes started to water. Mum and Dad didn't understand a thing, but they decided I must be shocked at seeing the picture and that John was laughing hysterically because he'd just seen my breasts.

When I went to bed later that evening, I was still feeling paranoid, and when Monday came around I didn't want to go to school. In the end, Mum and Dad had to follow me there, and when they dropped me off at the gates, I pleaded and begged them, "Can you come in with me, please?"

But Dad pepped me up and said that things would only get worse if I didn't put myself through it, and next thing I knew I was walking across the playground alone. Honestly, it was one of the worst things I've ever had to do. I can still remember the feeling in my stomach, the way my heart was racing. I mean, I never dressed provocatively; it was more the opposite. As far as I can remember, I usually wore pullovers and other things that covered me up. No one but my mum had seen my breasts before that spread, but now everyone was suddenly staring at me. I could hear the boys saying, "Oh, my God!" and things like that behind my back, and someone had pinned up the picture of me on the wall in the sixth form common room.

All that day, my heart raced in my chest. I felt so ashamed I could barely look anyone in the eye. But the students and teachers were actually pretty cool about it to my face. Apart from the head teacher, who was so angry that he called Mum and asked her to come into school the next day.

Mum told me how she had to sit patiently and listen to him complain that I had caused a great deal of anxiety among the first-years and then suggest that I should think about leaving the school immediately.

As far as I could tell, I didn't cause any anxiety at all. Actually, I was suddenly incredibly popular, so popular that before I went home one of those days, I had to sign autographs for a few boys in the corridor.

The fact that the head teacher was so angry probably had less to do with the picture, or even the pupils, and more to do with the fact that his surname was also Fox. He explained to Mum that he was constantly being called up by journalists and modeling agencies who thought he was my dad. The head teacher was really old-fashioned and hadn't actually seen the front page himself. He nervously asked Mum whether I had at least been wearing a body stocking in the pictures. Mum calmly replied, "Of course not," and continued, "If I'd found my daughter a job at a bank you would be happy . . . A modeling job clearly isn't good enough for you."

On the whole, the reactions were positive. People would stop me on the street and say that they had their fingers crossed for me to win the competition. It was a bit like becoming a star overnight, at least around the streets where I lived, and soon the *Islington Gazette*, the *Hornsey Journal*, and the *Haringey Independent* had all written about me. As far as the competition itself was concerned, the *Sunday People* printed updates on the various semifinals several times a week. Eventually, there were only three of us left, under the headline "Our Magnificent Three."

I finished in second place, which was obviously a bit annoying—particularly when I found out why I lost. Back then, I used to bite my nails, and the wife of one of the editors at the *Sunday People* thought it was ugly. Her name was Eve Pollard, and she was a well-known journalist and TV personality in England.

But now, looking back, where I finished actually worked out to my advantage. The girl who won has been practically invisible ever since. And if I had come first, I would have belonged to the Mirror Group. Instead, the Sun Group took the opportunity to chase me.

Around that time, a notorious serial killer called Dennis Nilsen was arrested, and a photographer by the name of Nigel Cairns went to his house in Muswell Hill to take pictures of the corpses and body parts being pulled up out of the drains. Nigel knew I went to school in the area, so he and a female journalist called Sian Davies went into the playground and started asking for my address and phone number. No one could or would give them the information they wanted, but someone said that my friend Ann Mole worked at a motor spares shop further down the street. Not long after that, Ann rang me up and said, "The *Sun* are here; they want you to do page three."

By this point, Dad had finally, after many long conversations, managed to convince the head teacher to let me stay on at school. I was hoping to study graphic design at college and needed to finish my art A-level. So I had just gone back to school when it was time for Mum and me to go a photo shoot at Beverley Goodway's studio, which wasn't far from Hatton Garden. I was sure that Beverley would be a woman, so I was surprised to say the least when the door was opened by a man who looked like a doctor. He had huge glasses and was really posh. Not at all like I imagined a glamour photographer.

Anyway, I remember that he asked us to come in and was very polite the whole time we were there. I remember it was a pretty quick photo shoot, too. To begin with, he took a picture of me without any makeup, wearing jeans, and then he took a topless shot.

Once we were finished, he said that before they could say when, or even if they would print my pictures in the paper, they needed to check whether it was legal to publish that kind of picture of a sixteen-year-old. Every evening after that, Dad and I went down to

Kings Cross just to see whether I was on page three. I never was, and I soon started to think it was because I was too young. I was actually pretty downhearted about the whole thing.

In the end, Dad's friend David Osten drove me into town. But instead of taking me to Kings Cross, he drove straight to the *Sun* offices, strode over to the pictures desk, and said, "I'm Samantha Fox's godfather and I'd really like to know if and when her pictures are going to be in your paper." They replied with something like, "They will be; we can't say exactly when, but she'll notice it when it happens."

What they said was true, because when Dad and I went down to Kings Cross like usual the next Saturday evening, we saw my picture splashed across the whole of the front page.

That was it for my studies. The head teacher expelled me. I was allowed to take my A-levels in art and music, but I wasn't allowed to stay on for the exams in any of the other subjects.

The Sun got such a response from their readers after they published that picture of me that two editors called Paul Button and Dave Chaplan called up Dad and wanted to take us out to lunch. When Mum, Dad, and I met them in the restaurant a few days later, they offered a mean exclusive four-year contract—the first such contract for any page three girl. So, honestly, I wasn't really all that bothered about not being able to go to school anymore. Though now, in hindsight, it does seem incredible that it was as a model that I would be starting my working life. Not because of my height, or even my lack of it. I'm thinking more about my childhood.

2

MORGAN MANSIONS, 1966-1976

The kids stared at me like I was some kind of
bizarre animal and shouted "Limpsy" at me.

My very first memory is an explosion and the smell of burnt flesh. I was two and a half, and I was at Nan and Granddad's house. Mum and Dad had been arguing again. They did it so often that Mum kept a bag packed and ready in the hallway. With it in one hand and me in the other, she would move in with her parents in Aberdeen Park on Highbury Grove. She was standing a bit away from me in Nan and Granddad's bedroom, folding the washing, when she heard the powerful bang. Since I was shaking, she thought I was having a laughing fit at first, but then she saw the sparks all around me and rushed over to try to unwrap the wire that had twisted around my burning hand.

I'd been playing with the switch on one of the bedside lamps. I managed to unscrew the actual button and got a real shock, and after that there was another bang. Mum pulled me away in panic, quickly wet a flannel and wrapped it around my hand. She grabbed me in her arms and hurried out of the kitchen. Nan and Granddad didn't have a phone, so she couldn't call for help. Instead, she ran next door, to the flat where a GP lived, and he called an ambulance. It only took a few minutes to arrive, and once they carried me inside the paramedic took off the wet flannel. The smell of burnt flesh washed over me again, and I lost consciousness.

Several years after the event, I could still remember the smell. The memories of my stay at Great Ormond Street hospital, on the other hand, are far more fragmentary. I know that Dad was there when I woke up. He'd come to the hospital as soon as he heard what happened. The doctors had operated on my hand and had been forced to take skin and tissue grafts from my legs and stomach. There would be many more operations as my hand grew, and I really did suffer during those hospital stays. Still, it's something completely different that etched itself into my memory. I'm looking out the window on one of those days and see Mum and Dad walking away from the hospital, hand in hand. My entire being is filled with some kind of calm. Because I realize, right there and then, that they'll be friends again.

They got married young. Mum was only eighteen and Dad twenty. He had a steady job as a bellboy in a hotel, dressed well, and was experienced in the ways of the world. Maybe that was what attracted Mum, whose great passion was dancing. Whenever she got the chance, she would dance in front of artists like the Rolling Stones and Dusty Springfield on a TV program called *Ready Steady Go!* She later went to an audition with the program presenter, Cathy McGowan, and was actually offered a permanent dancing role on the show. But since she was pregnant with me by then, she had to give up her dreams of a life in the spotlight.

They say that you don't really know someone until you live with them. That was something Mum discovered just a few days into her new married life. As though someone had flipped a switch, Dad became violent and controlling. But he had no reason to be. Mum never went behind his back, and she couldn't divorce him, either, because he controlled the money—including everything she earned. If she wanted anything, she had to ask for it and then show him the receipts for whatever she bought. Sometimes, even the receipts would send him into a rage, at least on those occasions when she bought something for the house and he didn't like it or thought it was unnecessary.

Dad was a minimalist, and he wanted few but expensive things. Everything had to be the best, the finest. Probably because he'd never had anything as a child.

My dad loved me; I know that. We were very close, particularly when I was little. But he had trouble controlling his temper and his feelings, and even if Mum bore the brunt of his violence, he did sometimes hit me, too. Mum would scream, "Not in the head, Pat, you can't hit her in the head!" And when he did it anyway, all hell broke loose. After a fight like that, up to six months could pass before they spoke to one another again. Six months without exchanging a single word. So in that respect, I suppose you could say I always felt quite insecure. I never knew when they would start arguing again, how far it would go, if we would run off to Nan and Granddad's or if we would stay. On one occasion, Mum and I even moved into a social housing flat. Something serious must have happened that time, because we lived in that place for almost a year.

To begin with, Dad often came over, but they would immediately start screaming at one another, and at one point he grabbed her by the neck. I'll never forget that, the way her eyes opened wide and she was almost gasping for air. I was completely overwhelmed by such a surreal feeling that I went cold and froze. Eventually, I rushed over to the fireplace. There was a white vase on the mantelpiece where I used to keep sweets. I grabbed it and managed to throw it right at Dad's head, and it fell on his toe.

Nan and Granddad never liked him, and I can understand that. If he was having one of his bad days, he was really awful. But he could also be the best dad in the world. Every weekend when Mum and I lived in that flat, he would come and pick me up to take me to educational places, places he thought I should know about, like St. Paul's Cathedral and Buckingham Palace. Over time, he taught himself carpentry and started his own company. I would go to work with him and help him with the filler or by painting first coats, and he would give me some pocket money for it. We went to the football, too, all of Arsenal's home games. I was a typical tomboy, never wanted dolls or dresses for my birthday—I'd rather have football boots, footballs, or guns. In a way, I was the son Dad never had. He had a season ticket, but there was a section called "schoolboys" where all the small boys could get in for a pound. So I would go in there and then climb over to his section and sit on his knee all match.

It was Dad who gave me my name, too. If I had been born a boy, I probably would have been Sam or Sammy. Instead, I became Samantha, after the main character in Dad's favorite TV series, *Bewitched*. Though to my family, I would always just be Sammy.

I have green eyes and blonde hair. But when I was born at Mile End Hospital in London on April 15, 1966, just a few months before England won the World Cup at home, I had dark hair, brown eyes, and a dark skin tone.

I was very small and thin during my first year, and I slept a lot. But the minute I learned to walk, I underwent a complete personality change. I became incredibly curious and was always touching things, and when we went to see my other nan and granddad in their little house in Clacton-on-Sea some weekends, Mum would have to keep an eye on me at all times. My other nan was quite a strict, strange woman, and it was only much later that I realized that she, probably just like Dad, was bipolar. It wasn't exactly something you talked about back then, but she understood herself well enough to check into a day center or home whenever she felt like she was going to have a bad turn.

Dad's mother had moved from Sheffield to London when she was young, and worked as a chambermaid in Claridges, where she met my granddad, who was a night porter at the same hotel. He came from Ireland and was considerably older than she was, and he was an alcoholic. So whenever he wasn't working nights at the hotel, he would usually be down the pub, drinking away their money. Occasionally, he sold the furniture from their studio flat to buy more booze. It was in that flat that Dad grew up, and he slept on the sofa in their living room right up until he married my mum. That kind of thing obviously leaves a mark on a person, and when I think about everything he did to me and to Mum, I want to believe there's an explanation for it in his childhood. Above all because it would make things easier for me now, looking back.

In any case, my mum's mum was the polar opposite of my paternal grandmother. Nan, as I always called her, was a funny, warm, and incredibly strong woman. She came from a family of traders, at Chapel Market in Islington, going back several generations. Nan's mother had a small shop there selling delicacies. Her brother Charlie had a magazine stand full of international newspapers. And Nan's sister's husband had a fruit and vegetable stand where I sometimes helped out as a child. Since I was so small and sweet, I used to be sent out to persuade the customers. I would hold out an orange as big as my hand and say, "Want to buy an orange, sir?" with my sweetest of little-girl smiles. I actually got a bit of money for it, too. But I could also get money just by turning up at the market. I often went there with Nan, and we would always bump into some relative like Uncle Charlie, who would press a ten pence piece into my hand, close my fingers around it, and say, "Go and buy yourself an ice cream, Sammy."

I loved that lively market environment and all the sounds, colors, and smells that went with it. I also loved to listen to the grown-ups talk. Sometimes, I even preferred to sit with them rather than play with kids my own age. Especially when Nan and Granddad talked about the war, about rationing and the ration cards they'd had to carry, about the Blitz, and—best of all—about Granddad's adventures. Granddad had been in the parachute regiment, a sergeant major, and wore one of those handsome red berets. During the battle of Arnhem, he was shot twice in the leg and ended up in a German prisoner-of-war camp with the rest of his platoon. The camp was in Poland and the prisoners were treated terribly—a German guard smashed Granddad's teeth with the butt of his gun, for example—and eventually Granddad and the others decided they'd had enough and escaped. They managed to make their way through Poland without being discovered, down through Europe, all the way to Italy. During this time, Nan received a letter saying that her husband was missing, presumed dead. It took a long time before she found out he was actually alive, and she never quite forgave him for going off to war. Especially considering he hadn't actually had to, given his relatively old age.

That uncertainty Nan had been forced to endure meant that sometimes, when Granddad's exploits came up, she would shout, "For God's sake, Dan. Stop going on about that bloody war!" Or sometimes she would just groan, "Here we go again about the war."

It's no exaggeration to say that my entire childhood was characterized by a number of catastrophes, big and small, and when I turned five and started primary school, it was time for the next one. I'd had another operation on my hand, because as it grew they needed to take more skin from my stomach; despite that, I couldn't quite straighten my index finger. As a result, I had trouble learning to write. The other kids picked on me because of it; meanwhile, Mum noticed around the same time that I ran a bit weirdly, too. It was almost like I jumped and lurched forward. When she asked me why, I said that it hurt and touched my hip. Straight away, Mum took me to the doctor.

The doctor looked at me and asked, "Does the pain keep you awake at night?" I shook my head, because it didn't. He examined me anyway, though he couldn't find the cause of the pain. I was referred to the x-ray department at University College Hospital, where they discovered I had something called Perthes disease, which meant that one of my legs wasn't developing like it should. They told us that I couldn't put too much strain on the bone and that I would have to wear calipers for two years.

I wasn't quite old enough to understand what all this meant. But I could see from Mum's face that she was really shocked, and I heard her take a deep breath when then they asked whether she and Dad wanted to enroll me in a school for children with polio. Mum and Dad talked about it that night, but both agreed that it would be best for me to stay at my current school. Clearly they thought I was strong enough to handle it. You had to be pretty strong to go to school in Islington wearing a pair of awkward metal calipers around your leg, and an equally awkward platform shoe on one foot. The whole thing was held together with leather straps and some kind of knee pad. You could really hear it when I walked—Mum told me that the entire stairwell echoed whenever I went up or down the four flights of stairs.

As luck would have it, my friend Debbie had broken her leg in three places and was forced to wear a cast for almost a year. We used to have what we called limp races, and could laugh at ourselves and one another.

But at school, and above all on the playground, things were different. The kids stared at me like I was some kind of bizarre animal and shouted "Limpsy" at me. It meant I got into fights pretty often. Like the time a boy mocked me for my big shoe and then pushed me so I lost my balance. As soon as I got back onto my feet, I kicked him in the balls.

Mum was called into school and asked me, sounding surprised, "How could you kick him, Sammy?"

"He teased me and tried to push me over," I replied angrily.

Another time, there were two boys shoving me. I grabbed them both by the hair and held them away from me until a teacher came running. Again, Mum was called into school. When she asked me why I'd pulled their hair, I told her the truth once again, that I had just been defending myself.

Mum looked at the teacher as we stood by her desk, and said, "Surely she has to be able to do that? She was defending herself and being beaten by two boys."

"Do you really think so, Mrs. Fox?" the teacher said, sounding outraged and pointing to the bin, which was full of large clumps of the boys' hair.

In the end, I got used to the bullying, or more accurately I stopped caring about it so much. It bothered me more not to be able to run about like the other kids, or join in whenever they played football. I couldn't take part in P.E. classes or play in the children's pool at school. But worst of all was that I couldn't go for bike rides with my friends, or follow them on adventures. Just before the doctors gave me my diagnosis, I'd wanted a bike more than anything for Christmas, and I got it, too. But by then I was already wearing the calipers, and my mum and dad had to sell it.

Something else that annoyed me about those calipers was that one of the leather straps gave me sores right at the top of my thigh, and if any pee got into the sore when I went to the toilet, I just wanted to scream. I didn't have to wear them at night, at least, but I wasn't allowed to walk or stand on my own. Dad had to carry me up and down from my loft bed. In the mornings, Mum would come with me to school, or more accurately she would push me there in a pram, because it would have taken me far too long to get there otherwise. When my little sister Vanessa was born—I was six at the time—Mum still had to wheel me to school, meaning she had to push two prams in front of her. It must've been incredibly hard for her.

I still did everything I could to take part in school activities, and I got to be the Virgin Mary in our nativity play. I'll never forget how, when I staggered onstage with a Jesus doll in my arms, I saw a couple of parents in the front row feel so sorry for me that they buried their faces in their hands and cried. When things got really bad, I used to think about what Dad had promised me once the calipers came off—that we would go down to Tower Bridge and throw them into the river Thames. And even if it always felt like that was an eternity away, the day finally came around.

Neither Dad nor I said anything in the car on the way to the Thames, or while we walked out to the middle of the bridge. I remember it was windy, and that I thought it was a bit horrible to have all the lorries thundering past. Above all, I was scared of the river itself. We stopped in the middle of the bridge, right where the two parts met, and I could see the dark, swirling water far below when the gap moved and widened by my feet. All the same, I was obviously excited, and once we threw the calipers into the water, I shouted in delight and clapped my hands.

One good thing did actually come out of the calipers. Just like the other accidents we lived through, they helped keep the family together. Mum, Dad, Vanessa, and I were all living together again. There was nothing I wanted more—even if Mum and Dad did continue to argue. When they were at their worst, Colin was often there, at least. He was the nephew of Mum's hairdresser, Lindsey. When Mum said she was looking for a babysitter, Lindsey suggested him. Colin was in his teens, and you didn't exactly have to be Sherlock Holmes to work out that he was gay. His feminine manner made him an easy target for the bullies at school. Plus, his parents weren't all that happy to have a son with that particular orientation. So he started hanging out at our place, and in the end he practically moved in. I thought it was great. Dad and Vanessa liked him, too, and Colin virtually became part of the family.

I've always had a great need to keep moving, and once the calipers came off it was like I wanted to do everything I'd missed out on. Every afternoon, I ran around outside like a madwoman. I also learnt to swim and dive, played football and netball, started gymnastics, and won a number of prizes at competitions. Something else that happened that spring of 1973 was that Dad decided we should go on our first beach holiday, to Hammamet in Tunisia.

Vanessa was still a baby at the time, so she stayed at home with Nan and Granddad. And since I was only seven, I can't say I remember much of the trip, other than one fairly crucial event.

At our hotel, there was a band that played every night. I loved listening to them and dancing on my own in front of the stage, and since the guys in the band saw me there night after night, one of them eventually asked if I wanted to sing something.

Next thing I knew, I made my first real appearance on stage. I have no idea what the song was, but I remember being full of nerves and excitement, and I also remember the roaring applause when I finished. Of course, it was hardly like a star was born that night, but I'd been bitten by the showbiz bug and was so exhilarated that Mum couldn't help but notice. So when we got back to Islington, she started scouring the papers for talent competitions I could take part in. She would read through a local paper and say, "Ah, there's a singing contest in Alexandra Palace this weekend. Think we should go?" I always did. In fact, there was barely a single talent show that I didn't take part in. But it wasn't just the singing that interested me. At school, the teachers couldn't keep me out of the school plays, and it wasn't long before Mum let me go to an audition at Anna Scher's theatre school. I got in and started going there in my spare time, along with stars-to-be like Phil Daniels or the Kemp brothers, Gary and Martin, who would later conquer the world in Spandau Ballet. Anna Scher herself was an incredible teacher, and we spent a lot of time doing improvisation. She could see every student's personality and allowed it to come out. There were no Shakespeare plays on the schedule; it was all the kind of thing we young people could relate to and understand. I really was spellbound by the theatre, or maybe it was by standing on stage and being given applause. There was a magic to it that I just couldn't put my finger on.

3

CROUCH END

Two girls around my age came walking down the other side of the road, but they barely looked at me. They seemed a bit stuck up, which bothered me.

On my tenth birthday, April 15, 1976, we moved from Morgan Mansions to Crouch End in north London. Dad had long wanted to get us out of Islington, which was pretty rough at the time, so I'm sure he thought it was great. But for me, it was like moving to another world, or at least like moving to a village in the countryside. None of the tube lines ran to Crouch End, just the W7 bus.

Where I grew up, almost everyone lived in council flats. In Crouch End, most people lived in small houses of their own. We wouldn't have had enough money to buy one of them if it hadn't been for a private property company getting in touch and offering Dad a mortgage if we moved—they wanted to convert our old council flat into two flats.

In any case, the whole area just seemed a bit more posh. Even kids were different. I noticed it immediately when I went out to play on that first day, while Mum and Dad unpacked boxes inside.

Two girls around my age came walking down the other side of the road, but they barely looked at me. They seemed a bit stuck up, which bothered me. Not long after that, a red-haired boy appeared. He seemed to be about the same age as me, too.

"You new here?" he asked, looking me up and down.

"Yeah," I said. "We moved in today."

I'd recently been given both glasses and a brace, and I mentally prepared myself to be laughed at for it. But instead, he said, "You look like a midget. I bet you're a midget."

Yes, I'd always been told that I was small. But there was something in that boy's attitude that made my blood boil. From a young age, Dad had taught me how to defend myself. "If someone hits you, you hit back even harder"—that was his advice. And then he taught me how to box.

As far as that boy was concerned, he didn't even need to touch me; it was enough for him to repeat "Midget!" for me to see black and throw myself at him.

At almost that exact moment, Mum looked out of the kitchen window to shout that dinner was ready and saw me sitting on the boy's chest, hitting his face, which was now bleeding.

The fact that I exploded like that probably wasn't just down to that boy's superiority. Just a few weeks earlier, it had suddenly been time for the next family catastrophe. In our old flat, there were nice wooden panels on the walls in the living room, and after we'd emptied all the furniture, Dad said, "Those have to come with us." He asked me whether I wanted to help pull out the nails. I was used to following Dad around when he was out on jobs, and I always thought it was fun to help out, so I was soon sitting there with a pair of pliers in my hand, coaxing out nail after nail. Vanessa wanted to help, too, and was picking up the nails from the floor that had fallen there.

Suddenly, I heard her scream. The sound was awful, and I knew immediately that something serious had happened. A wooden splinter had flown off the wall and hit Vanessa straight in the eye. She was holding it with both hands and screaming. I went cold and didn't know what to do. Mum came running, and next minute she and Dad had run out to the car with Vanessa while I was frozen to the spot with anxiety beating in my chest.

Vanessa went blind in that eye and—just like me with my hand—would have to undergo a series of operations as she got older.

My dad never forgave himself, although it was a million-to-one chance that it happened.

Starting a new school is always daunting. But I don't think I was ever as tense as I was before I started at St. Gilda's. For one, it was a Catholic school, and pretty strict, and secondly, we would be taught by nuns.

At my old school, I'd always been able to play the class clown. I would pull funny faces behind the teachers' backs or get up to other mischief without any real consequences. But at St. Gilda's, there was zero tolerance for that kind of thing.

During my first week there, a nun asked me to spit out the gum I was chewing in class. I remember I pretended to hide it in a piece of paper. But at break time, while I was blowing a bubble in the corridor, the same nun spotted me again and rapped my legs with a ruler. A few weeks later, we went on a school trip and were meant to be collecting frogspawn in glass jars. I didn't think it was much fun, so I started kicking stones into the water instead. Next thing I knew, I felt a stick whip across my legs. The fact was, they hit me quite a lot in the beginning, those nuns, at least until I learnt to drop my Islington attitude and got into line.

But what worried me most about starting that new school was that I would have to be baptized. Dad was Catholic and Mum belonged to the Church of England, but neither of them was especially religious or went to church on Sundays. As a result, they hadn't bothered to get me baptized as a Catholic. But now, suddenly, it had to happen, because you couldn't go to St. Gilda's unless you had been baptized—that was just how it was. Father Dennis was the one who would do it, and he thought that the ceremony could take place in the classroom with all the other students standing in a ring around me. I couldn't think of anything more embarrassing. It wasn't made any better by the fact that the two witnesses who were meant to stand by my side during the ceremony—one of Mum's friends and one of Dad's—never turned up. But what could I do other than let Father Dennis dip my head in the water in front of my classmates, who were standing in a ring around us, hand in hand, their mouths open?

I was still going to different talent shows with Mum, and it was around this time that I bought my first single on vinyl. I got hooked on the song when I heard it on the radio, but I had to work up the courage to go down to the record shop and whisper, rather than ask the assistant, "Do you have 'Love to Love You, Baby' by Donna Summer?"

There was a rumor going around at school that it was a real orgasm you could hear Donna having on the record—and when I put it on at home, it didn't take long before Mum appeared in the doorway wondering what I was listening to. "Good song, isn't it?" I said, doing what I could to look as innocent as possible.

Soon after that, I started at a new drama school on Mountview Road, the Mountview Theatre School. Just like everything else in that part of town, it was a bit posher than I was used to. My cockney accent also meant I always ended up playing the same kind of roles in every production.

I was involved in a number of plays at St. Gilda's, too, and I remember the nativity play that year in particular. Father Dennis had written it, and when he gave me a role, I was completely beside myself, though my excitement was dampened slightly when I realized that—probably because of my accent—I would be playing one of the Pharisees. A villain, in other words. Anyway, the Pharisees were meant to walk around with some kind of box on their heads, so they could keep fragments of the Dead Sea Scrolls in them, and Mum covered a big matchbox with gold paper and fastened it to my head with ribbon.

In those days, all the schools competed to be the one with the best nativity play. The winner that year would get to be on TV, and that turned out to be us. Not that the BBC broadcast the whole performance, just parts of it. But you could clearly see me walking around with that gold box on my head, shouting, "That man should die!" about Jesus over and over again with real feeling.

Afterwards, I was interviewed by a local newspaper and asked what I wanted for Christmas. I remember I said, "A Crossfire game"—one of those rapid-fire shootout games where you shot at one another with red plastic guns and small metal balls. Like I said before, I was a real tomboy, and when Dad gave me that game for Christmas that year, it was the best present I'd ever gotten.

Another typically boyish thing I liked was making go-carts using wheels from discarded prams, with string to steer them. There was a long, steep slope not far from our house, and I used to ride the go-carts down it without being able to brake. Once, that meant I crashed straight into the door of an off license. But the time I really remember is when I put Vanessa in the front, gave it a run-up, and then jumped in behind her. I suddenly felt an intense pain in one leg, and when I looked up I saw a couple of boys from my school sitting on the embankment by the old railway tracks, shooting at us with an air rifle. I heard *poff, poff, poff,* and next thing I knew they had hit my other leg. Out of sheer panic, I tried to protect Vanessa by leaning as far forward as I could at that high speed. She was already blind in one eye, after all, and I could just see myself trying to explain to Mum and Dad how I'd made her lose her sight in the other one, too.

The air rifle darts continued to whizz past our heads, and once we'd finally made it out of shooting range and I'd stopped the go-cart by steering it into the edge of the pavement at the bottom of the hill, I was in a cold sweat and shaking all over. I could barely feel the pain from the darts that had hit me, but I know that I ran home as fast as I could, dragging Vanessa by the hand, and told Dad what had happened.

He looked at the four air rifle darts with different-colored feathers that had gone through my jeans into my legs. Without a word, his eyes completely dark, he stormed outside. A while later, he came back with three of the boys and two air rifles.

"Are these the ones who were shooting at you?" he said.

Vanessa and I both nodded. Dad turned back to the boys.

"Drop your trousers!"

The boys looked at one another, but they didn't dare do anything other than what he told them. Dad continued, "Against the wall!"

The boys turned around, and Dad picked up one of the air rifles. Then he shot the boy to the far right in the leg. The boy screamed. Without flinching, Dad shot the two others, who also shouted and whimpered. Then he said, "Now you know how it feels." He made me tell him where the boys lived, and he visited all their parents. They ended up being suspended from school.

I would later get an air pistol of my own, but I kept it secret from Mum and Dad. I never thought of using it to shoot anyone; I just messed around with it and played bull's eye with metal cans up on the same embankment the boys had shot me from. Actually, I just liked playing up by the abandoned railway tracks, which you could follow all the way to Highgate.

As for Vanessa, she didn't seem to understand how serious what had happened on the embankment was. Everything had happened so quickly, and I hadn't let on how much it hurt when the darts hit me. I really did manage to protect her that time, only to unintentionally hurt her deeply two weeks later.

By that point, Vanessa was at the same school as me, and there was going to be a fancy dress contest—a competition where you dressed up as whatever you wanted. Mum had rented a really nice Andy Pandy costume for her, and Vanessa was completely over the moon with it. For once, I had no desire to take part myself, and I told Mum as much. But on the morning of the competition, it was like something came over me—a sudden urge or a small devil of some kind. Mum was waiting in the hallway with Vanessa, who was wearing the Andy Pandy dress and eager to get to school and the competition she hoped she would win.

"Wait, Mum, I just need to do something," I said, running upstairs.

Mum sighed loudly and shouted after me, "We don't have time to wait for you, Sammy. What's so important?"

But instead of replying, I rushed into Mum and Dad's room and put her rollers into my hair, blackened one of my teeth with shoe polish, wrapped a scarf around my head like a turban, and stuck one of Mum's cigarettes into my mouth. I pulled on the flowery overcoat she wore for cleaning and stuffed my feet into Dad's old leather slippers. And just as Mum and Vanessa were about to leave, I came down the stairs looking like a caricature of a cleaning lady and grabbed Mum's mop and bucket. They both stopped dead and stared at me with wide eyes.

On the way to school, Vanessa didn't say a word. Mum didn't seem to know what to say, either. I just remember feeling incredibly pleased with myself—and when I made my entrance onto the stage in front of all the pupils and teachers, I shuffled forward with my hand on my hip, squinted towards the judges, and said, "Allo, darlings, I've just popped in to tidy up."

Everybody laughed and loved it. I won, of course. Vanessa came second and was completely crushed—though in a pretty stiff-lipped way.

By this time, Mum had long since stopped keeping a bag packed, moving in with her parents, or running to another flat on a regular basis. But that by no means meant that she and Dad argued any less. I remember one time in particular, a few nights after that competition. Vanessa, Mum, Dad, and I were at the dinner table, eating fish and chips. Mum and Dad weren't talking. They didn't even look at one another. Suddenly, without warning, Dad grabbed the bowl of chips and threw it against the wall. Mum started to scream, and then Vanessa did, too. Not really thinking about what I was doing, I jumped up from my seat and grabbed Dad around the throat from behind. He pushed me away and left the table, and Vanessa, Mum, and I continued to eat dinner in silence.

The next morning, once Dad had gone to work and Vanessa had left for school, I heard Mum groan in the hallway. When I went out to her, I saw her suddenly bend double. Next thing I knew, she was on the floor, crawling and bellowing. I was completely paralyzed. But she was staring up at me with her eyes wide, a helpless look in them—and that was when I realized I had to do something. I ran to the phone and called a neighbor, because that was the only number I could remember. The neighbor gave me the number for the emergency services, and though my mouth was so dry I could hardly talk, I managed to phone for an ambulance, which then seemed to take forever to arrive. Eventually, Mum made it to the hospital, where they discovered she had a serious case of gallstones and needed an emergency operation. It's a routine operation that isn't meant to involve any complications, but something went very wrong. Mum ended up in intensive care, and she came close to kicking the bucket.

A few days later, when Dad and I went to visit her in Whittington Hospital in Highgate, he told me, "Don't be scared when you see her."

That turned out to be easier said than done, because when I came into her room and saw how thin and pale she was, how many wires she was hooked up to, I immediately started howling. In the end, Dad had to ask me to leave. He didn't want Mum to get upset, because that might make her even worse, and I guess he was right. Still, it took several visits before I could control myself enough to go in and see Mum and give her the smile she needed so much.

As a result of various complications, Mum ended up staying in hospital for several months. I would cry whenever no one could see or hear me, and I struggled to sleep at night out of fear she would die. Dad was always at her side, and whenever he wasn't, he was working. In other words, I was left to look after the house. I was only eleven, but I had to learn how to cook, clean, and do the washing in no time at all. As far as I can remember, it went pretty well. Taking care of Vanessa was much worse. Considering we're sisters, we're very different. I almost never argued with Mum and Dad. Vanessa, on the other hand, wasn't anywhere near as obedient and didn't seem to care if she got punished. It made no difference whether I threatened to tell Dad that she wouldn't go to bed—she just stared at me with that stubborn smirk of hers and repeated, "I'm still not going to bed."

"I swear, I'll tell Dad when he gets home."

"Do it, then," was all she said. She really did drive me mad, that girl, and I later came to realize that in many ways, she was like Dad and my other nan, his mother. The same stubbornness, the same tough indifference that sometimes gave you the feeling you were trying to grab hold of a perfectly slippery, smooth stone. Now, looking back, I also realize she had always been jealous of me, and maybe above all of my close relationships with the family. But in a way, it was her own fault that she fell out with everyone. I mean, I used to go to see Nan because I wanted to see how she was. Vanessa never did that kind of thing. She didn't care, never called to see how any of our older relatives were doing. I was Nan's favorite because I always cared about her and loved her deeply.

I cared about our even older relatives, too. Granddad's mum, for example, always wanted me to go and visit her in the old people's home where she lived. So I went there a lot, and on her birthday, just after Mum came out of hospital, I took the bus over there to give her flowers and chocolate. She was so happy and wanted to give me a sherry. She'd clearly already had a few glasses with her friends, who were sitting in her cozy little room, all talking loudly and laughing. I was still just a child and had never tried alcohol before. But because she forced it on me, and because the mood was so happy, I took the glass she handed to me with the words "Go on, have a sherry." As soon as I drank it, she refilled the glass, and my head soon started to spin.

My great-nan clapped her wrinkled hands and shouted happily, "Come on, Sammy, give us a song!"

The other old ladies joined in: "Yes, give us a song, Sammy!"

I started singing songs I knew they liked, songs that Mum and Nan had taught me, and they soon started singing along. They filled my glass again, and everything started spinning even more.

When I finally left, I was so far gone I could barely find the way out. I felt incredibly sick, and had to try hard not to throw up on the bus home.

4

STEPHEN MORIARTY

My fate in life is, and has probably
always been, to cheer people up.

I was fifteen when I first noticed the effect I had on men. It was on the beach during a holiday in Florida. Mum and Dad had gone off to look around the shops while Vanessa and I stayed on our towels. I've always loved sunbathing, and I dozed off on my back. I didn't notice what was going on around me. But when Mum and Dad came back a while later, they couldn't see either of us for all the boys crowding around the spot where we'd been when they left.

It turned out that was just the beginning. When we got home to London, boys and men continued to give me attention I wasn't used to, without me trying to show off any of my physical attributes at all.

I was at the St. Thomas More Roman Catholic School by this point, which was in Haringey, not far from Crouch End—and which, like St. Gilda's, was a school with nuns for teachers. But despite the strict religious routine, it suddenly became popular for the boys to stand and wait for me whenever I had detention, which unfortunately happened every now and then. It wasn't that I had trouble learning. It was more that I had trouble paying attention in subjects I wasn't interested in. And then I would start talking or getting up to mischief like putting drawing pins on the teachers' chairs, or sticking notes saying *I have yellow teeth* or *I've got BO* on their backs.

Something else I had to get used to around then was the small line of boys that often formed, wanting to follow me to the bus at the end of the day. When we did a production of *Grease* at school and I was cast as Olivia Newton-John's character, I got called to see the headmaster. I remember he cleared his throat a few times, gave me a serious look, and said, "You can't be quite so promiscuous onstage."

I had no idea what "promiscuous" meant, so I didn't say anything. But as soon as I left his office, I went straight to the nearest pay phone and called the house to ask Mum.

"It means you're sexy," she said without hesitating. That was, without doubt, one of the best things about her—that we could talk about anything and she would always tell it like it was. I'll never forget when I was about to start at St. Thomas's, for example. I was only eleven, but she went through all the essential facts of life with me, everything from how people got pregnant to how I should dress. Since I wasn't interested in skirts and dresses, or rather had no idea how a girl or woman was expected to dress, Mum took care of that for me. In terms of clothes and makeup, she's pretty much always been my opposite. When she was young, she was super trendy and really into the whole Jean Shrimpton look. She used to wear long false eyelashes, lots of powder, and thick, black eyeliner to finish it off. She looked incredibly glamorous and elegant, and to me she was always the most beautiful woman on earth.

Anyway, back then I had a weekend job in the fruit and vegetable section in Tesco, and even there I noticed a change. The men and boys who came in suddenly started taking forever to buy a pound of carrots, apples, or potatoes.

On the same street as Tesco, there were some small photo shops, and on several occasions while I was walking to work, amateur photographers came over to me and wanted to take my picture. All in all, it meant I developed a feeling that there was something special about me. I just had no idea what. Now I know precisely what it is, and it's actually very simple: my fate in life is, and has probably always been, to cheer people up.

But even if I got a lot of attention, I'd never actually been with anyone. I'd never even been asked out on a real date. The only experience I had in that regard was that I was secretly in love with one of my teachers. I'd even invited him to my birthday party when I turned fifteen. But he was mature and smart enough to pretend it had never happened. Mr. Chandler, another teacher, sadly didn't have that same level of judgement and used to make smutty remarks when no one else could see or hear. But the real winner was the male teacher, who would lift up my skirt and slap me on the bum, or keep me behind after class to stare at my breasts or harass me in some other way. I remember thinking he was really horrible, but I never told Dad because I was afraid of what he might do. In any case, I didn't know a thing about dating or love, and maybe that's why I reacted the way I did when, one day when I got off the bus on the way home from school, a cute guy spoke to me.

He was hanging around outside Stroud Green Fruiterer's (another of the greengrocers in the area) with a cup of tea in his hand, and he gave me an appreciative look, smiled slightly, and said, "Can I offer you a cup?"

I was so surprised that I didn't know what to say and just kept on walking. But when I got home, I told Mum what happened. She laughed and suggested I go back and buy her a few pounds of potatoes from the shop. So, the next day, I went back there and came out with butterflies in my stomach, because the boy had asked me out on a date for that evening. His name was Stephen Moriarty, he was a couple of years older than me, and he was manager of the shop. And pretty soon after that, he became my first real boyfriend.

We went dancing at the clubs in Wood Green, but only until ten o'clock, which was when Mum and Dad said I had to be home. We went to restaurants sometimes, and to the cinema, where we could kiss and make out. But we never slept together, even if we did try a few times. I remember that we took baths together and did what we could to get in the mood by watching *The Postman Always Rings Twice*. Still, it never happened, because I always found it painful. I just wasn't ready.

After a while, in any case, I started working at Stephen's shop at the weekends, rather than at Tesco. This must have been at some point in late autumn 1982. Because, as far as I can remember, I was wearing a thick winter coat while Mum and I waited for the bus one afternoon. We'd just visited Nan and Granddad. By that point, I was so used to boys and men staring at me that I barely even noticed the two boys driving down the street on their mopeds. They were practicing for their taxi exam and trying to learn all of London's streets.

The one in the lead spotted me, his eyes went wide, and he smiled. The one behind him turned his head, too, and drove straight into the back of the moped ahead of him. It was a proper collision, and next thing I knew they were both lying on the ground next to their mopeds. People came running, and we ran back to Nan and Granddad's flat and called an ambulance for them. I had a strange feeling that somehow, it was all my fault.

5

SAM-MANIA

At home I was just Sammy, a sixteen-year-old virgin in tracksuits, and at work I was Samantha Fox, Great Britain's top pinup.

After I came second in "The Face and Shape of 1983 Contest" and signed that four-year contract with the *Sun*, I quickly became a phenomenon in Britain. The headlines said things like "Sam Storm," "Play It Again Sam," and "Sam-Mania." All the papers wrote about me, and cards and letters from readers wanting to know more about Samantha Fox started pouring in to the *Sun*. Most of them were from men and boys. But there were also some from women who had been following and cheering me on during the competition, and I soon realized I just had to play the role. I mean, at home I was just Sammy, a sixteen-year-old virgin in tracksuits, and at work I was Samantha Fox, Great Britain's top pinup.

It's true that I had dreamed of being a singer or an actress. But now that I'd been given the chance, I planned to seize it and become the greatest page three girl ever known.

In our house in Crouch End, the phone rang nonstop. Dad eventually had to get another line just for things relating to work, and from March 1983 onwards, I was doing personal appearances (PAs) virtually every day. I opened shopping centers, bars, and bingo halls, that kind of thing. And the fact that I was quickly fully booked was probably also down to me making as much of myself as a glamour model as I could. I mean, if I went away to do a PA, I always made sure it became a real event. They wouldn't get some tired model turning up in a taxi, dressed in some cheap dress. Samantha Fox sent sparks flying, and she always arrived in a rented Bentley with two bodyguards dressed in black suits. It was a bit like KISS at the beginning of their career, when they used their small fee to buy empty amp boxes, which they put on stage for effect, or to rent a limo to drive them to and from the show. Though it didn't take long before I really did need the bodyguards. The pressure of the crowd wanting an autograph or picture with me after these events was sometimes so big that once I had to flee from the roof of the shopping center in a police helicopter, and several organizers were forced to call the whole thing off to guarantee both my and the crowd's safety.

Just three months earlier, I'd been an ordinary schoolgirl. But now, people turned to look at me wherever I went, and a whole load of admirers started trying to make contact with me in various ways. I remember one guy in particular, because he left a plate of homemade food outside our door every day. In the end, Mum got sick of it and wrote a note saying, "Sam's on a diet," which she taped next to the door handle. Not that it stopped the guy. Instead, the very next day, he left a plate of Caesar salad on the step.

I was actually getting so many different job offers that I was forced to turn the majority of them down. One that I said yes to, despite everything else, came from Chris Brough, who was a fairly heavyweight music producer, publisher, and manager. Around that time, he was managing people like Shakin' Stevens and Showaddywaddy. Anyway, Chris had seen the pictures from the Face and Shape of 1983 competition in the paper and wanted me to go down to a club in Knightsbridge to audition for a new pop band he was forming, a band he was calling Replica.

I'd kept the dream of becoming an artist myself one day there in the background, so of course I went down there.

I remember that there was a long queue of girls outside the club, but since Chris had invited me down there personally, I didn't have to wait with the others. Instead, a girl called Melanie and I were asked to stay behind. We got to sing for Chris's friend Steve Roland, a music producer, and the next week we did a test recording of a song called "I Like Plastic" at Red Bus Studios. It was never released, and Replica never took off. But Chris did become my manager, and I was offered the role of singer in a new band called SFX. Chris even arranged a contract for two singles with Lamborghini Records.

Chris had a pleasant manner and a huge amount of experience in the entertainment industry, music in particular. Maybe that was the main reason I fell in love with him. He was forty-six at the time, with a wife and kids. I was seventeen.

I know it might sound weird, but I've always liked older people, have always been drawn to people who can teach me things. And soon enough, it was plain that Chris was in love with me, too. Obviously, that wasn't in any way ideal, and it was far from easy to bring up with Mum. I would never have dared talk to Dad about it. I didn't even dare think about what he would do if he found out.

But, like I said before, I could talk to Mum about anything, and I can clearly remember the moment I dropped the bombshell. It was late one night, during the week. I was sitting on the bed in my room when she came in to say good night. I looked down at the floor and then just came out and said it, barely opening my mouth.

From the corner of my eye, I saw her freeze.

I threw my arms in the air.

"I love him."

"No, you don't!" Mum lowered her voice before she continued, "Are you having sex with him?'

"No, but I want to."

Since Mum knew I would do what I wanted regardless of what she said or did, she took me to the doctor the very next day and put me on the pill. And the whole way home, she said, "Don't you dare tell your father about this!"

It took six weeks before the contraceptives had time to work. But then the moment finally came. We were in a flat belonging to Steve

Roland, in Maida Vale, West London. It was probably like the vast majority of first times—no big deal, in other words, and over and done with pretty quickly.

As far as that flat is concerned, we actually took my first modeling card headshots there. I also went there to rehearse songs I would be recording. Chris's friends, who didn't take long to work out what was going on, made fun of him for falling for a teenager. But far worse than that was his wife, Sharon Brough, who was also my stylist for the headshots, walking in on us kissing in the living room at their house.

Sharon clearly had had her suspicions about what we were up to for some time, particularly when Chris suddenly started working out like mad and bleaching his hair. But she had tried to keep it at a distance. That wasn't possible anymore, and so she took their daughter, Joanna, moved in with her parents, and sold the story of my relationship with Chris to the press.

That was how my dad found out about it. And I probably don't need to say that he went absolutely apeshit.

Chris and I were on what we were officially calling a PR trip when it happened, and when we got home he said he wanted to explain it all to my dad, face to face. I told him it wasn't a very good idea. But Chris wouldn't listen, and not long after that we were standing in the hallway at home like two criminals who'd been caught red-handed—and before Chris had time to say a word, Dad had launched himself at him and pushed him up against the wall. Somehow, Chris managed to escape through the front door, but he phoned me up the very next day and said, "I think we should actually leave things here."

I remember I took it hard. I mean, I'd never been dumped before. So I shut myself up in my room and cried my eyes out.

What happened next was that Chris made some bad decisions relating to my career, and Dad wanted me to completely break off my relationship with him, which I did. Not long after that, Chris was in a car accident. He broke his back and was paralyzed from the waist down. Roughly ten years ago, he took his own life.

But before all that happened, we had time to release two SFX singles, "Rocking with My Radio" and "Aim to Win." The former was written by the guitarist in Ian Gillan's band, Gillan, and the latter by Theresa Bazar from the pop duo Dollars. Ringo Starr's son Zak Starkey actually played the drums on "Aim to Win." It featured the keyboard player from Classix Nouveaux, too. And even though neither of the songs were smash hits and SFX never really took off, my first tentative steps as a singer had given me a thirst for more.

Now, looking back, I would probably say that it was lucky my music career didn't take off right then. I was fully booked both day and night, and I did my first overseas job that summer, in Antigua in the Caribbean.

It was me and four other models, and I remember that I wanted Mum to come along. For some reason, she couldn't. Maybe we couldn't afford it; maybe she needed to look after Vanessa—I don't actually recall. What I do remember is that the minute I met up with the other models in Heathrow, I immediately felt like an outsider. They were older, more experienced, wore great clothes, and had Dolce & Gabbana bags. I was still just seventeen and was wearing a hoodie and a pair of tracksuit bottoms. My bag was a huge, awkward Samsonite. And even though the other girls were nice and did everything they could to make me feel OK, I remember that I cried when the plane took off and that I felt completely empty when we arrived at our rented villa on the beach in the middle of the night.

The next morning, I also discovered that the villa was in the middle of nowhere, far away from absolutely everything, and that there was no phone. But the fact that the house was isolated from civilization did actually turn out for the best, because once the girls and I had eaten breakfast, the idea was that we would work on our tans. In other words, we had to sunbathe naked so we didn't end up with any tan lines.

One of the girls who had been in the industry for a while took out a bottle of baby oil and told me to smother myself in it. She said it would help the sun to take better. Since we only had two days to work on our tans, and since she was more experienced than me, I did as she said. Sure enough, the sun took better with the oil on my skin. The problem was more that it took a bit too well, and within a few hours I'd burnt my bum so badly that I could barely sit down.

The pictures would be taken by two different photographers. One, called George Richardson, turned up on the very first day. George worked for Rex Features, a huge photo agency. His job was to take a load of different topless pictures, which would then be sold through the agency. The other photographer, Leslie Turtle, arrived once we were done with George. Leslie was known for taking naked pictures, and the contract (which my dad had carefully gone through) stated that his images would only be published outside of the UK, using a fictitious name. I mean, Dad and I had never even considered that one day I might be world famous.

Even in photos that you might have thought would reveal everything, I managed to hide my right middle finger, which even today bears some damage from that explosion when I was little. In fact, I didn't show it—or the scar on my stomach—once during my career as a glamour model. Looking at the pictures today, you can see that I always have the damaged finger pulled back, and that my index finger is always hiding my scar.

Anyway, in Antigua, we were being photographed one girl at a time. The others were dozing in the sun, and as I lay there waiting for my turn, a black guy with dreadlocks suddenly appeared on a horse. Since we were completely naked, he obviously couldn't help but stare, and when he spotted me, he shouted, "Sam! Sam! I'm from Islington . . . We met a few years ago in the Hope and Anchor!"

I sat up, and while he talked, I tried to use my hands to cover myself as best I could. It turned out he knew my whole family and was in Antigua on holiday.

Right then, Leslie shouted over from the spot where he was taking pictures, "You know that kid, Sam?"

"Yeah," I shouted back.

"Ask him if we can borrow his horse tomorrow."

The next day, the boy with the dreads came back with the horse. The only problem was that it didn't have a saddle, which meant that it wasn't all that easy to ride, particularly not when you were stark naked like me. Plus, my whole bum was sunburnt. I did my best anyway, and Leslie snapped a few pictures. After a while, he stopped and seemed to be thinking about something. Then he told the boy with the dreads to let go of the horse's reins, as they were visible in shot. The boy did as Leslie asked, which he shouldn't have, because the horse whinnied and then took off at a gallop with me clinging to its back. I'd never ridden a horse before, and I have no idea how I managed to stop myself from falling off. Once the initial shock subsided, I tried to work out how to get the horse to stop. It really was going fast, and I felt a wave of panic wash over me. Maybe that was why I tried digging my heels into its sides to slow it down. Anyone who's ever ridden will know that this had the opposite effect. The horse was running so fast that the palm trees and bungalows were rushing by, and suddenly I was in a tourist area. There were families with children sunbathing all over the beach, and I could see the British men and women turning their heads and asking, "Isn't that Samantha Fox?"

By this point, I wasn't just scared of hurting myself. I was painfully aware of how naked I was, and so when the horse started to run out into the water I just jumped straight off. Unfortunately, the water was only about a foot deep, so I managed to bash myself quite badly. By that point, people had started to crowd around on the beach, and everyone was staring at me, so I just nodded apologetically and tried to cover myself with my hands as best I could.

"There you are!" Leslie said, sounding unconcerned, when I managed to make my way back some time later. He explained that he wanted to take some pictures of me sitting in a palm tree. Since I was so young and inexperienced and wanted to seem professional, I didn't say a word about what had happened, or about how much pain I was in; I just obediently climbed the tree Leslie had picked out. There was no doubting that he was happy, because he praised me nonstop while he clicked away. It was only once he finished that we realized neither of us had any idea about how I should get back down again.

In the end, Leslie had to run over to the house to look for a ladder. My entire body was aching, the sun was blazing, and every minute felt like an eternity.

After at least an hour, he came back with a rope in his hand and threw it up to me. I tied it around my waist and managed, after a lot of to-ing and fro-ing, to lower myself down.

Around this time, there were new pictures of me in the *Sun* almost every week, and though my contract meant that they were the only ones allowed to print my topless shots, the other papers still published daring pictures of me. As a result, there was plenty of talk back home and within my family. Nan, who was there when Mum took that first picture of me for the Face and Shape of 1983 competition, was nothing but supportive. When she saw me topless on the front page of the *Sun*, she would say things like "Ah, your hair looks great!" And whenever I went shopping with her, even when she promised she wouldn't do it, she couldn't stop herself from pointing to me in the shop and saying, "Guess who this is! It's Samantha Fox, my granddaughter!" And I would stand there, wearing no makeup at all, with a baseball cap pulled down on my head, not knowing quite where to turn.

Granddad was proud, too. He liked to bet on the horses, but only small sums of money. Every time he went away to bet, he would take newspapers with pictures of me in them and tell people, "That there's my granddaughter."

Dad was quite split about the whole thing to begin with, but after his colleagues and friends told him they were proud that a girl from our neck of the woods had done so well, he found it easier to accept what was happening.

The only person around me who wasn't happy about my career was my other nan. She didn't comment on the pictures; she didn't ring me; she just blanked me out.

Since I'd been forced to end my relationship with Chris, Mum and I started looking for a new agent or manager.

I remember that we contacted all the big modeling agencies. The first one we met with was an agent called Samantha Bond (who later became known for representing Katie Price). Mum and I sat down with her in her office. She was a real heavyweight even back then, and she had a good reputation. But it wasn't a long meeting. The first thing she said to me was, "You're too small." The second was, "You'll only do well in porn." Mum was so angry that she grabbed my hand and said, "Come on, we're leaving!"

After that, we met another agent called Geoff Wootten, who also thought I looked very young—like a little girl. He suggested another agency called Tiny Tots.

"OK," said Mum. "But maybe you want to see her pictures first?"

Mum showed him my portfolio, and as he looked through it, he said, "Oh . . . wow . . . uh . . . hmm . . ." and suddenly he wanted to work with me. But we didn't like him, so we left.

It was Yvonne Paul who ended up representing me. Sadly, the jobs she sent me on were mostly for swimwear and things like that, where the models were meant to be incredibly tall. It was like she didn't care or quite understand what kind of model I was. After a couple of failed auditions, Dad called her and shouted at her, which I can understand. I was having to attend auditions where they were looking for fashion models, leaving me feeling embarrassed. No one could understand what I was doing there.

Dad said, "You're sending her on the wrong kind of casting."

And Yvonne replied, "If you think you know better, Mr. Fox, then you can look after it yourself." And that was when Dad got into management.

6

SPRING 1984

"You need to make a proper go of this now, and put your career before everything else. Because you've got no more than six good years as a model, remember that."

I was on the sofa watching TV when Dad appeared from the office he'd set up for himself on the ground floor of our house in Crouch End.

"Sammy, another geezer just phoned; he wants you to open his shop on Saturday. I said it was fine. It's actually a bit of a way from the other opening you're doing, but so long as the traffic's not too bad we should make it in time."

Dad was talking faster than usual, and he headed back downstairs before I had time to say anything. I honestly don't know when things became like that, but I'd noticed that ever since he became my manager, we never talked about normal things anymore—just business.

I looked out of the window and sighed. It felt like everything suddenly revolved around the character of Samantha Fox. Not just when I was working and stepped into the role, but at home, too. Thank God my Mum was still my Mum and cared about her little girl. That very moment, as though to prove it, Mum came out of my room and said, "Sammy, I've worked out what you should wear tomorrow!"

"Great!" I said, trying to smile.

Mum looked pleased and left the room to sort out my clothes. She really did everything she could to make things easier for me back then, and whenever I felt down or even just a bit tired, she would say, "You need to make a proper go of this now, and put your career before everything else. Because you've got no more than six good years as a model, remember that. I'll take good care of you, my darling, and be there with you."

She was right, of course, but at certain times I still felt sad that our family was now more like a business.

The front door slammed shut.

"Hi," Vanessa said, casting me a quick glance before she disappeared into her room.

Even she was affected by my fame. Mum had told me that at school, the others would say things like, "Why aren't you as hot as your sister?"

Having to deal with that as a twelve-year-old must have been hard. Not that she showed it, but I knew she wasn't as indifferent as she tried to make out, because I would occasionally find my clothes in her wardrobe and see that someone had been using my makeup. I did feel sorry for her, and she did get bullied, which I'm sure affected our relationship.

The sun had peeped out from behind the clouds, illuminating the living room wall, and my mind was racing. I mean, inside I still felt like the same old Sammy who spoke with a cockney accent and liked fish and chips and football.

That said, it was a while since I'd last played for Arsenal's girls' side, though I'd always spent more time on the bench as a result of various injuries—many of the other girls came from borstal schools, and they played fast and rough. Dad and I never went to matches together anymore, either. But I was Arsenal's mascot, which meant I sometimes got to hand out checks for good causes during halftime at Highbury. And one day I got a phone call from the club's official photographer, Doug Paul. He often came over to the house to do short interviews with me for the local newspaper where he also worked, the *Islington Gazette*—which called me "our girl"—and we had become kind of friends.

"I've got a great idea for a photo shoot," he said. "What do you say about having your picture taken with the Arsenal lads during one of their training sessions?"

Two days later, I found myself standing among the club's star players, people like Graham Rix, Charlie Nicholas, and Kenny Sansom.

The boys didn't exactly seem to have anything against me being there, and I made eye contact with Kenny Sansom, who wasn't just handsome and charming, he also played for England. Once the session was over and the pictures had all been taken, he asked me out, and the minute my granddad heard that I was being courted by "the golden boy," as Kenny was known back then, he was over the moon.

Granddad was a fanatic Arsenal supporter, so he made sure he was at our house when Kenny came to pick me up for that first date. He waited by the window, and the minute he saw Kenny pull up outside, he practically ran to the front door, shouting over his shoulder, "I'll get it!"

Poor Kenny found himself being dragged into the living room, offered tea, and subjected to a cross-examination by Granddad about why this or that had happened in the last few matches, what he thought about the upcoming fixtures, which tactics the team should be using, and so on.

"Please, Granddad, we need to go now," I eventually said. The look of relief on Kenny's face was huge. All the same, I was glad that Granddad had got the chance to meet him. It was something he would love talking about later, with relatives and friends.

Where does a top footballer take a girl on their first date? Well, Kenny drove straight to Highbury, where there was an Under 21s match on, and took me in as a VIP guest. Lots of girls probably would have been disappointed with that, but since I loved football, I thought it was great to go there with him.

We did things more by the book on our second date. He came to pick me up in a limousine and handed me a red rose as he opened the door.

"Can I offer you a glass of champagne?" he asked as he sat down next to me.

"Yes, please," I said, thinking that this probably topped being in the stands at Highbury.

Kenny turned on a Johnny Mathis record. Mathis was clearly his favorite, because he didn't play anything else the whole way to the nightclub. He sang along, too.

Tramp was a super-exclusive members' club where people like Prince Andrew used to hang out, and it felt special to be let in. We soon ended up at a table full of Kenny's friends, his teammates mostly.

One of the specialities at Tramp was that they served sausage and mash with your name written in the potatoes, basically a posh sausage and mash. Fancy or not, I ordered it anyway.

When my sausage arrived, Graham said, "Bet that's the biggest sausage you've ever had."

Kenny immediately flared up, grabbed Graham by the shirt collar, and slammed his head against a wall light.

"I should bloody well kill you," Kenny hissed, looking like he meant it.

For a minute or two, I—and plenty of the others—thought that a full-blown fight was about to break out between the Arsenal players. In the end, the others managed to calm down Kenny—and Graham, who then spent the rest of the evening glaring at him. But just as I managed to relax and started toying with the idea of being Kenny's girlfriend, Charlie Nicholas came over.

"Hi," I said, flashing him a friendly smile.

"Listen . . ." He cast a quick glance over to Kenny, who was at the bar getting us more drinks.

"Yeah?"

"What do you say about going out one night?"

"You and me, you mean?"

"Yeah." The way he said it made it seem so obvious, and I felt my jaw drop slightly. I didn't know quite what to say.

"That . . . would probably be a bit weird . . . since me and Kenny . . ."

"Yeah, yeah, I know, but think about it anyway?" He smiled, as though it was the most natural thing in the world to come on to his friends' girls, and then he left, right before Kenny came back with our drinks.

"What did Charlie want?" he asked.

"Nothing special," I said, avoiding Kenny's eye. "He told me a joke I didn't really get . . ."

"Yeah, that Charlie's a real joker," Kenny said, sipping his drink.

"Mmm," I said, suddenly feeling a sense of unease that didn't really disappear until Kenny and I left the club and got back into the limo at three in the morning.

Like before, it was Johnny Mathis the whole way home. And again, Kenny sang along. But suddenly he went quiet and kissed me—until I almost lost my breath. Then he looked me deep in the eyes and said, "Sam, there's something I need to tell you."

"Aha," I said, feeling the unease come rushing back.

"I'm married."

And with that, it was as though all the feelings he had just awoken in me vanished. I didn't want to be anyone's toy. I wanted to feel like I genuinely meant something to whoever I was with.

There were no more dates with Kenny after that, and I didn't see him again until much later—at a charity cricket match I was taking part in. He was in the crowd, and after the match he unexpectedly came up to me and said, "Hi, Sam, it's been a while." I initially didn't recognize him. His face was all swollen, and his entire body was shaking.

"It's me . . . Kenny . . ."

I almost started to cry. He had looked so good at one point in time, but now the drink had really taken a toll on him—and, it turned out, he was broke. He told me that he had gambled away all the money from his professional career, which reminded me of another big footballer I used to know, George Best. Like Kenny, he was incredibly charming and kind, and we could talk about football for ages. He was always so impressed that I, a girl, knew so much about the sport. I never once saw him blind drunk, but that's the way it is with a lot of alcoholics—they never really seem that drunk. It's only when they stop drinking that you realize they've got a problem.

I bought myself a brand-new Mini sports car with some of the money I earned that spring. Not that I could do anything but admire it parked up outside the house, because I still didn't have a driving license. I had actually started taking lessons, but I failed my first test. I don't want to blame anyone, but one of the main reasons was that I was being hounded by the press. I mean, it's not exactly easy to keep your nerves in check and do everything right while a load of paparazzi are following behind you in cars and on motorbikes, constantly taking pictures.

The same thing happened when I took the test again in early summer. It really was annoying.

When I got home that day, there was a knock at the door. I'd just taken off my makeup and was lying down on my bed when Dad came in and said, "Sammy, there's a journalist here, from the *News of the World*; he wants to talk to you about your driving tests . . . He's offering quite a lot of money for an exclusive and for joining you during the next test."

I groaned but then quickly composed myself and went out into the living room, where I met a man with curly hair who introduced himself as Kit Miller. I recognized him. He was an entertainment columnist—or more accurately a gossip writer—but he was known for having good relationships with a lot of celebrities. He sat down in an armchair opposite me, and after Mum brought in some tea we started to talk. I quickly realized that talking to him had put me in a better mood.

A few months later, he came along to my third test. Sadly, I blew it again. Afterwards, Kit and I went to a pub to do a new interview.

Once we were done and he was about to leave, I asked whether he wanted to come to a small family gathering we were having that evening.

"Sure," he said, which made me happy, because I had really started to like him.

We went on a date a few days later, but he didn't even try to kiss me. I wondered to myself whether it was because I was "Samantha Fox" or because he was literally twice my age and didn't have the nerve. In fact, it was more because he was a real gentleman, and it wasn't until our third date, as we were on the way to a film première one evening, that he finally summoned up enough courage to make a move. He had been quiet for a while when he suddenly grabbed me and pushed me up against a parked car. And then he kissed me, a little too hard. Once it was over and we started walking again, he didn't say anything for a long time—almost as though he was shocked by what he'd just done.

"Is everything OK?" I eventually asked.

He didn't meet my eye when he mumbled, "Absolutely."

Maybe his behavior was a bit strange, but I just thought he was sweet. It didn't take me long to realize that he was also incredibly romantic. He often sent me flowers, and if I woke up alone in bed after we spent the night at his flat, I might find a note next to me reading, "I love you."

Kit was newly divorced when we first met, and he had a son who was Vanessa's age. He drank too much, and for the most part nothing happened when we shared a bed. If I'm completely honest, we were more like good friends than lovers. In fact, as far as I can remember, we didn't sleep together more than three times during our entire relationship. It took me a while to realize that Kit was an alcoholic, which seems a bit strange looking back. I never saw him properly drunk, but I should have been able to work it out all the same. I mean, back then, most Fleet Street journalists were more or less based out of one of the pubs along that street, and Kit was no exception. But I guess I was so used to people drinking that I didn't realize that when Kit pretended his hands were shaking because he was "starstruck," he really was shaking.

Around this time, I was getting quite a few strange job offers. I said no to a lot of them, but I was also very aware that my time as a model was finite and that I had to strike while the iron was hot. That's why I sometimes said yes to things without really thinking them over. One example was a photo shoot for *News of the World*.

They wanted me to go to Brighton to open England's first real nudist beach. The reporter they sent with me, Simon Kinnersley, wasn't quite as used to being naked as I was, but he had no choice. The idea was that we would spend an entire day on the beach, and that meant nudity was required.

Even though I often appeared topless in pictures, I wasn't entirely comfortable doing it around a whole load of other nudists. In fact, as I took off my bikini bottoms there on the beach, I slightly regretted saying yes. Still, I tried to look as relaxed as I could as the photographer snapped pictures of Simon and me posing with huge beachballs in front of our most private body parts.

Once the photographer was finished, I put my bikini bottoms back on and we lay down on a towel to sunbathe. People were passing by constantly, some of them fully dressed. They really just wanted to get a look at me.

Just as I lay back down, the sun was suddenly blocked out by something, and when I opened my eyes all I could see were a pair of huge, hairy balls dangling above my face.

"Can I have your autograph?" I heard a gruff male voice ask.

"Sorry?" I said, trying to make out anything other than the terrifying balls hanging in the air like the weight from an old clock.

The man leaning over me was in his sixties, and other than the dark blue sun hat on his head, he wasn't wearing a scrap of clothing. I was only eighteen at the time and hadn't seen all that many naked men, but the sight of him hardly made me want to see more.

"I was wondering whether I could have your autograph," the man asked again, and then he coughed, which made his entire package tremble.

I didn't know what to say or where to look.

"I don't have anything to write with—or on," I eventually said with a shrug.

The man grunted unhappily and waddled away.

A few weeks later, I found out that I had won the *Sun*'s Page Three Girl of the Year poll, and that I'd done it by a landslide; a full two-thirds of readers had voted for me. I could barely believe my ears when my name was read out to the crowd of celebrities at Stringfellows.

In any case, that award raised my status as a model, but it also meant that men became even more obsessed with me. One of them was Tony Curtis, the Hollywood actor, who started coming on to me and my model friend Debee Ashby one night at a club called Bootleggers. Tony was fifty-nine at the time, and Debee was one year younger than me, only seventeen. I enjoyed talking to Tony, since Mum and I used to watch his films. I even asked him where his daughter, Jamie Lee Curtis, had bought the sexy black pants she wore in the film *Trading Places*. I really liked them and wanted to wear them for a photo shoot. Tony said they were from a shop called Thrash in Hollywood, and he actually sent me a pair in the post.

I didn't find him at all attractive, however, and he was really old. The next morning, when I told Mum that he'd invited us to Los Angeles to stay with him, she said, "You're not going there. Blimey, he's too old even for me! Maybe he looked good at one point in time, but look at him now!"

But Debee thought that Tony's offer sounded tempting. And her mother had nothing against her daughter spending a week with a strange man who was old enough to be her grandfather. In fact, I heard her saying, "You go for it, girl!" on the phone.

7

LEMMY

I'd never drunk spirits before. I usually stuck to Buck's Fizz—champagne and orange juice, that is. But Lemmy drank Jack Daniel's the way other people drink water, and strangely enough he did it without seeming especially drunk. I got incredibly drunk, though. In fact, when Dad came to get me that evening, I was more wasted than I'd ever been or would be again.

In mid-February 1985, *Penthouse* published a couple of the naked pictures I'd shot in Antigua during my first year as a model, despite the fact that the contract had been clear: the pictures were never meant to appear in any UK magazines or papers. As I said before, when I did them, I never thought I'd be an international star.

The day the pictures were published, I was at my friend Christopher Biggins's house in London. We were talking about everything under the sun, like always, and it wasn't until I went to leave that I realized there were about twenty journalists and paparazzi waiting for me outside. At that point I still had no idea why they were there, but the cameras started flashing and the journalists began shouting over one another the moment I opened the door:

"Sam, you said you'd never pose naked. Why are you doing it now?"

"How much are *Penthouse* paying you?"

"Do you really think your fans want to see *everything*?"

I was in shock, and as I tried to get into the car with my bodyguard, Dave, who had come to pick me up, one of the photographers got so close that he managed to hit me in the face with his camera lens. I ended up with a huge bruise on my cheek.

As we drove away, I swore silently at Leslie (the photographer), who must have earned a fortune from the pictures. On top of that, Dad had already told me that a phone sex line was using my pictures in their ads without my permission. Suddenly, it felt like I was fair game, like anyone who wanted to could use me any way they liked, without any consequences.

The *Penthouse* publication did, at least, make me want to get away for a while. So Kit and I decided to go on holiday to Portugal with Mum and three friends. Not that Kit was having all that easy a time of it right then. It wasn't just that Mum was always keeping an eye on him; being with me also meant he had to deal with jealous men wanting to fight him whenever he was out and about in London's pubs and clubs.

But the biggest problem, as I said before, was that we were really more friends than lovers, even if I was hoping that the trip would bring us closer together.

Kit had said that the easiest and most exciting way to get to southern Portugal would be to fly to Malaga and rent a car there.

So, when we landed, the six of us squeezed into the little rental car with all of our luggage, and Kit started driving west. But the more time that passed, the more tense and irritated the mood became.

"Almost there," Kit attempted several times.

Eventually, no one believed him, and at one point even I couldn't stop myself from saying, "Nice road trip you've brought us on, Kit."

When we finally made it to our hotel after eight hours on the road, Kit seemed incredibly downcast, and not long after we got back to London, I realized that our relationship was unsustainable. So, one evening, when Kit and I were on the way to a new restaurant I was opening, I decided to end things.

Kit was used to me babbling almost nonstop, and he gave me a questioning glance as we walked side by side in silence. In the end, I said, "I think it's best if we don't see one another for a while."

Even though Kit had probably sensed what was coming, he stopped dead and looked like his world had just come crashing down around him.

"I mean, obviously we can still be friends," I said in an attempt to calm him down.

But Kit just cried, and I really did feel sorry for him. I stroked his arm and said, "Come on, let's go."

The next day, Kit apparently ripped down all the pictures of me from the walls in his office.

But right there and then, there was so much going on in my life that I didn't have time to brood over him. That entire spring of 1985, I was fully booked practically every day, from first thing in the morning until late at night. And while I barely remember even a fraction of all the things I did, I do clearly remember being on the jury in a spaghetti-eating competition that Capital Radio had organized at a restaurant called Ciao, on Belsize Lane in North West London, just a few days after Kit and I broke up. The competition involved eating a portion of spaghetti in the fastest time possible, trying to beat Peter Dowdeswell, the Guinness World Champion. The competitors' fees were being donated to orphaned and poor London youths, and Lemmy Kilmister from Motörhead was with me on the jury. We said hello to one another, and Lemmy told me that he was a massive fan. I'd soon find out just *how* big.

As we sat there watching people wolf down spaghetti, he asked whether I could sing. I nodded and told him that I had been in a band called SFX.

"Then I think we should do a song together," he said.

So one afternoon not long after that, Dad gave me a lift to Lemmy's flat in Kilburn. It must have been sometime in April, because I remember it was spring outside. I also remember feeling a bit nervous—Lemmy was a huge star even then. My nerves hardly got any better when he opened the front door and I stepped into the hallway and saw the huge collection of posters and photos of me on his walls, including one of the naked images of me from *Penthouse* a few months earlier. I quickly positioned myself so that Dad wouldn't be able to see it. I was worried that if he did, he wouldn't let me stay. But he didn't seem to notice, because all he said was, "I'll pick you up tonight, then!"

"Yep, see you later," I said with a forced smile.

Once Dad had gone, Lemmy showed me into the living room, where I got my next shock. He had literally covered the walls with pictures of me. In some of them, I was as naked as on the poster in the hallway.

"If we're going to work, we need a bit of inspiration," Lemmy said, going over to the stereo.

I don't know what I was expecting to hear, but it definitely wasn't what he put on—ABBA, turned up loud.

"I love this stuff! Incredible melodies!" he shouted to me.

I nodded in amazement, as I hadn't expected that.

"Want a drink?"

I nodded again.

Lemmy went over to the fireplace, and I noticed that there was a whole line of Jack Daniel's on the mantelpiece. He opened one of them, filled two glasses to the brim, and handed me one.

"Cheers!" he smiled and raised his glass.

I'd never drunk spirits before. I usually stuck to Buck's Fizz—champagne and orange juice, that is. But Lemmy drank bourbon the way other people drink water, and strangely enough he did it without seeming especially drunk. I got incredibly drunk, though.

In fact, when Dad came to get me that evening, I was more wasted than I'd ever been or would be again.

"Did it go well?" he asked, giving me a suspicious look.

"Yeah," I said, doing everything I could not to fall over in the hallway. Again, I had to hide the huge naked picture of myself. It took an almost superhuman effort, and the minute I got home and closed my bedroom door, I fell forward onto the bed and was asleep before my head even hit the pillow.

Mum and Dad obviously weren't so naive that they didn't realize Lemmy had given me alcohol, but I suppose they thought I could take care of myself. I was nearly nineteen, after all. Anyway, I continued to go over to Lemmy's place, and we really did write a song together, "The Beauty and the Beast."

"Couldn't really call it anything else, could we?" Lemmy said, grimacing into the huge hallway mirror in front of us.

I laughed, because like many other "hard" rockers, he was anything but a beast. In fact, he was a real gentleman and treated me with a huge amount of respect from the very first time we met.

We recorded a demo of the song on his four-track and then booked a session at a real studio to record it properly. Once we were finished, we were given copies of the track on cassette so that we could listen back to it at home and think about what changes we needed to make. But a few days later, I got a phone call from Lemmy. Just from his voice, I immediately knew something was wrong.

"We can't release the song."

"Why?" I asked, surprised.

Lemmy told me he was in a dispute with his record label, Bronze Records, and that he'd now realized he couldn't release material anywhere for the next five years.

"After we announced it and everything," I said.

Because we'd just had press images taken, and we had talked about it in the papers. We had even done a treatment for the video to go with the song. In it, Lemmy would be sitting with his back to the camera, wearing a blonde wig so that everyone thought he was me. But as I started to sing, he would turn around with a mad grin.

"These things happen," Lemmy said. He didn't sound especially concerned. He was quite a bit older than me and had plenty of experience in the music industry, something he often shared. In just a few weeks' time he would be going away on one of the endless tours that took up a huge chunk of his life, so I took the opportunity to ask him if he wanted to come to my nineteenth birthday party at Stringfellows before he vanished.

"Of course I do," he said, and he sounded genuinely happy to have been invited.

Among the 250 guests invited to the party were Würzel, the guitarist from Motörhead, Pet Shop Boys, Duran Duran, Spandau Ballet, a couple of page three models, some famous footballers, and Kit, who seemed to have swallowed his disappointment and accepted "just" being my friend.

It made me happy to see Mum and Dad dancing and having fun together again. But the real highlight of the evening had to be when a load of blokes tried to get into the club. A fight broke out, and my bodyguards, Dave and Mark, rushed over.

"Stay there!" Dave shouted to me over his shoulder.

Never, I thought, following closely behind.

Dave and Mark threw themselves straight into the brawl, and they quickly sent at least fifteen men flying with their kicks. It was like watching a Bruce Lee film, and I loved it.

"No match," Dave said to me, straightening his jacket with a smile.

The fight had put him in a good mood, such a good mood that not long afterwards, he suddenly got to his knees in the middle of the dance floor and placed two bricks on top of a couple of others.

The DJ lowered the music and the crowd formed a circle around Dave, who gave them a slight bow. And before anyone had time to work out what he was planning, he slammed his forehead into the bricks, snapping both in half.

Typical Dave, I thought to myself.

Because Dave really did like to be seen. He often made sure he was photographed next to me, and it was obvious that he wanted to be famous himself. That was probably why he'd decided to work with me in the first place. But I also think he wanted to be with me. Why else did he keep quiet about his wife and daughter, who he lived with in Camden? That was something I only found out later, from a friend, who also told me that Dave had made his wife deny they were even married. Until one day, when she decided that she'd had enough and divorced him.

But right then, he was in Stringfellows, soaking up the applause. Dad had moved over next to me, but he wasn't clapping. He didn't like Dave, and he thought that martial arts were for pussies.

8

DAVID CASSIDY

There was my childhood idol, sitting in front of a mirror with bulbs around the edges, his hair in curlers. When he caught sight of me, he quickly raised a hand to hide the small bald spot that was glowing in the light of the bulbs.

People always say that meeting your idols in real life quickly leads to disappointment. How true that proved to be for me in May 1985, when I suddenly found myself meeting one of my biggest childhood idols, David Cassidy.

I'd had David as a pinup boy on my wall and kissed him good night every single day. Like so many other young girls, I'd also had all of his records and loved *The Partridge Family*, the TV show he starred in. He was in England to try to revive his music career with the help of a PR guy called Gary Farrow, who also worked with bands like Wham! David had a new single out, "Romance," and when it came to releasing the title track as a single, Gary wanted them to do it as a picture disc with a Rudolph Valentino theme—in other words, depicting David as the great seducer. David's American manager loved the idea and asked Gary who the hottest woman in England was right then. The answer was me.

I didn't really know what kind of pictures they wanted, but when I got to the studio I was already made up and dressed. I always used to make sure I was ready when I arrived at a job, which was partly down to Dad thinking that the makeup artists often made me look like a Barbie doll or a tart. In any case, one person who wasn't ready was David. He clearly needed to spend a lot of time in makeup, and since we still hadn't been introduced to one another I went over to his dressing room to say hello. I remember I was both nervous and excited as I knocked on the door and was quickly shown in.

The sight that greeted me probably wasn't what I had been expecting. There was my childhood idol, sitting in front of a mirror with bulbs around the edges, his hair in curlers. When he caught sight of me, he quickly raised a hand to hide the small bald spot that was glowing in the light of the bulbs.

"I just wanted to say hello before we get started," I said quietly, taking an unsure step towards him.

David flashed me a forced smile and held out his hand, we exchanged a few polite words, and then I left him in peace.

Not long after that, it was time for the photo shoot, and we were told to strip from the waist up. David positioned himself right up close and leaned in as though he was about to kiss me, à la Valentino. Thank God, no boobs were showing, as it was all to be left to the imagination. I tipped my head back and looked up at the ceiling. It felt a bit stupid, but that didn't bother me as much as the fact that David had an erection.

Whenever he pressed himself against me, I could clearly feel his dick. He was also sweating buckets onto me beneath the bright spotlights, and when I cautiously glanced at his face, which was right next to mine, I saw the small, telltale incisions by his ears, revealing that he'd had a face-lift. David seemed to be deliberately drawing out the photo shoot, which took an eternity, and he had an erection the entire time—something he did absolutely nothing to hide.

Dad had come along to make sure everything went to plan, but I didn't dare tell him or even hint at what David—or rather a certain part of him—was up to. If Dad had found out, he would have gone crazy.

Once we finally finished for the day and the photographer (and presumably also David) had what he wanted, David asked whether I would like to eat dinner with him that evening. I gave Dad a look of uncertainty. Sadly, he didn't realize that he was meant to call the whole thing off, and instead he cheerily suggested that the three of us and Gary Farrow should go out together. I suppose Dad just wanted to make a good new business contact in Gary.

So, that evening, the four of us—me with some misgivings—went to the White Elephant, an exclusive restaurant on Grosvenor Road where celebrities like Rod Stewart and Britt Ekland often ate.

In the middle of dinner, I got up to go to the toilet, and as I was standing alone in the women's toilets, washing my hands, the door flew open and David Cassidy came storming in.

Before I really had time to process what was happening, he had pushed me up against the wall and his hands were all over me. I shouted, "Get off me, David!" in an attempt to stop him.

But instead, he just stuck his tongue into my mouth and shoved a hand under my skirt, while the other kept a firm grip on one of my breasts.

I reacted quickly and instinctively by bringing my knee upwards, striking him right in the balls.

David jerked back with an "Ouch!" and grabbed his crotch with both hands. I took a deep breath and shouted, "Get away from me!"

David looked up at me—he seemed almost surprised—and then I elbowed him in the face.

I guess I had my bodyguard, Dave, to thank for those self-defense moves, and as I rushed away, leaving David by the sinks in the women's toilet, he was standing with one hand on his nose and the other cupping his balls.

Back at the table, I sat down without saying a word. If I had mentioned what had just happened to Dad, he would have knocked David's lights out. In that moment, the handsome, sweet guy from *The Partridge Family* had transformed into a first-class creep who wasn't worth the risk of a stretch in prison. All he deserved was disgust, and when he came back to the table he avoided looking at me.

"You got a cold?" Gary asked him.

"No, why?" David replied.

"You keep touching your nose."

We finished dinner without either Dad or Gary suspecting a thing, and the next day Gary phoned Dad and invited the two of us to the première of a musical called *The Time* which David had been given the lead role in. It was originally supposed to be Cliff Richard playing "The Rock Star," but now David had replaced him.

"Could be fun," Dad said when he came out into the living room to tell me the news.

"Mmm," I said, choosing to keep quiet once again, even though I had absolutely no desire to spend any more time with David.

I managed to avoid it, since David pretended he hadn't even seen me in the crowd at the theatre after the show. His wife, on the other hand, glared at me, and I later read that she had accused me of trying to start an affair with him! When that happened, I had a good mind to ring one of the papers and tell it like it was. But I didn't. It just wasn't my style to fling crap at people, even if they deserved it.

In any case, the whole David Cassidy affair made me uneasy, so it felt good to head to Spain with Mum, Dad, and Vanessa a week or two later. We'd rented a house for three weeks in the mountain village of Frigiliana, about thirty miles from Malaga, and we planned to just take it easy. A photographer called John Kelly did come out to take some pictures of me for a magazine, but he and I got on so well that it didn't feel like an intrusion. Plus, the pictures turned out really well.

"Sammy, what do you think about the idea that bloke from Chelmsford mentioned?" Dad asked one day as I was sunbathing next to the pool by the villa.

The bloke from Chelmsford, whose name was Brian Jones, owned a printing factory that I had officially opened a month or so earlier. While I was there, Brian had suggested that I start a fan club. His idea was that I should hire him to print a calendar full of pictures of me, and on the back we would advertise my fan club, thereby gaining paying members. Making my own calendar also meant it would be me and only me who earned money from the pictures . . . money we could use to print posters, newsletters, and membership cards for my fan club.

"It is actually pretty win-win," Dad said, climbing into the pool to cool off.

No one at that time manufactured their own calender, and no page three girl had a fan club. If I had any doubts about the idea, they disappeared the minute we got home and saw the mountain of new fan mail in the hallway. Those letters were often just addressed "Samantha Fox, London," but somehow they had still managed to find us.

We really did need someone who could take care of all that mail, because I no longer had the time. I did still read the most important letters—the ones from fans who had been in accidents or who needed support of some kind—but I just didn't have time for the vast majority of the rest.

So Dad hired a photographer to take pictures for the calendar, and during the photo shoot I realized that I really had become a professional and knew exactly what was needed for a good result, and so did my Mum. Once again, she did the styling and made it look classy with amazing accessories and beautiful underwear. At one point, I said to the photographer, "If you want to be the calendar king, you'd better make sure you keep me focused!"

I have no idea if that was what did it, but the calendar turned out really well, and when it eventually went on sale it started to sell faster than Brian Jones could print new copies. His plan had been a success, and after just a few weeks my fan club had ten thousand members, each paying ten pounds for a year's membership. That included a signed photo, a quarterly newsletter, and the possibility of winning a night out on the town with me. The money the fan club brought in meant I could hire an assistant to deal with all the fan mail I got, as well as print the first newsletter and make T-shirts and all the other things we were planning to sell through the fan club.

At one point we had 10,000 members; then Brian Jones ran off with the money. That must have been the first—but definitely not the last—time I got ripped off.

One small comfort came at the end of August, when I was voted Page Three Girl of the Year for the second time, and again the prize ceremony took place at Stringfellows, with lots of my friends present. It was around this time that I also started presenting segments on a TV program called *The Six O'Clock Show*. It was a mix of news and entertainment, filmed in front of a live audience, and the TV people clearly thought I was doing a good job, because they offered me a forty-two-week contract. That, along with my appearances on talk shows like *Des O'Connor Tonight* and Terry Wogan, really did make me a household name in a way no other page three girl had managed.

One Saturday, I went to Essex to open a Mercedes car dealership. The guy who ran the place, which was owned by his dad, was called Jason Wright, and he was an ex–West Ham player. He was really handsome, and once I was done with the autographs, he came over to me and said, "Where does a guy like me take a girl like you?"

One of the more boring things about being me was that few if any men ever dared come up to me. So I liked that Jason had guts, and I replied, "Anywhere you like."

A few days later, he took me to a nice restaurant in central London, followed by a concert by the soul artist George Benson. Unlike my mum, I wasn't a huge soul fan.

"Good, right?" Jason said to me during the show.

"He's fantastic!" I lied.

Because even if the music wasn't quite to my taste, Jason was. Above all, I liked that he had courage and that he cockily told me he would be a millionaire by the time he was thirty.

Another thing I liked about Jason, which became even clearer as we continued to see one another, was that he wasn't at all interested in the world of celebrity.

"Do we really have to go there?" he would say when I told him we had been invited to a celebrity party somewhere. "There'll just be a load of bloody photographers there."

He was virtually the polar opposite of Kit, and sometimes I found myself wishing that I could be anonymous again. For a while, with Jason, that almost felt possible.

Sadly, the bubble burst once the press started terrorizing Jason's family. His dad phoned mine and complained that there were always journalists and paparazzi outside their house. Jason was annoyed by it, too, and things hardly got any better when his ex-girlfriend suddenly appeared on page three under the heading "Anything Sam Can Do, I Can Do Better!"

"I'm going crazy," Jason said as he stood with the paper in front of him. He shook his head and suddenly looked incredibly downcast.

In that moment, I knew that our relationship wouldn't survive the stress my celebrity put it under. And not long afterwards, he said to me, "Sam, this isn't working."

We sat down and came to the conclusion that it really would be best if we stopped seeing one another. Though it was good to avoid all the usual drama, it still felt sad that it was other people, not us, who were making it impossible for us to be together.

But, like always, I didn't have time either to mourn or to think all that much about what had happened, because just a few days later I was heading to the Austrian ski resort of Mayrhofen. I was going along with a few other page three girls and Beverley Goodway, who had taken my first photos for the *Sun* and would be taking pictures of us with some kind of skiing and Christmas theme for the paper.

The whole thing sounded incredibly simple. At least it was until we landed, when Beverley, who was also acting as our group leader, needed to hand out our passports and started reading out the names on them. Since all the girls—other than me—used fake names, he was constantly having to ask who each of the passports belonged to. We had to repeat the entire procedure when the lift passes were handed out. Everything seemed to take an eternity, and the job itself turned out to be both cold and difficult. The idea was that we would pose on the ski slopes in just our knickers, boots, and Santa hats. But there were people passing by and staring at us the whole time, and there was a ski lift right above our heads. As I stood there, so cold that I was shaking, trying to smile at Beverley, I would hear people above me saying, "Look! Isn't that Samantha Fox?"

Unlike some of the other girls, I was at least used to skiing and didn't fall over constantly or get my skis crossed. One of the girls, Kelly, had never even worn a pair of skis before, and Beverley wanted her to squat down on the slope while he took pictures.

To begin with, everything was fine. Kelly squatted down and smiled at Beverley, who encouraged her and gave her instructions on how to twist her body so it looked like she was going down the slope. The only problem was that she soon started doing just that.

Her skis started moving by themselves and Kelly was struck blind by panic when she realized she was heading down the hill and had no idea how to stop. She let out a piercing scream and continued to squat down as she picked up speed.

The remaining girls, Beverley, and I just stood there with our mouths open, and we saw a faint yellow trail begin to appear behind poor Kelly, who was so scared that she had wet herself.

The other skiers on the slope below us were also staring at the girl in the thong and Santa hat who went flying past them, screaming at the top of her lungs.

She did at least manage to stay upright, and when another girl and I quickly pulled on our sweaters and headed down the slope after her, partly to give her something to cover herself up with, partly to see if she was OK, we just followed the yellow trail on the snow.

We found Kelly curled up on the ground. She was ashamed and shaken, but we got her into her sweater and dried her tears.

The day I got back to London, Mum and I went to the première of *Back to the Future* at the Empire Theatre in Leicester Square. There had been a lot of hype around the film, and the entrance to the cinema was crawling with celebrities when we arrived—even Prince Charles and Princess Di were there. Even so, the people behind the barriers went wild when the chauffeur opened the door and I stepped out onto the red carpet.

In the beginning, I found going to premières completely nerve-racking. My legs went all wobbly and my mouth went dry. When the photographers' flashes started going off and I smiled my biggest smile, my upper lip would start twitching uncontrollably.

That uncertainty also meant that I didn't really know how to handle the cameras. So rather than starting at the left and methodically working my way to the right when all the photographers shouted my name, I would stare desperately in every direction. In any case, it didn't take me long to realize that I needed to learn the rules of the game, and the person I learned most from was Marilyn Monroe. I mean, she really gave the cameras what they wanted, pouting her lips in a kiss or leaning forward and showing off her décolletage, for example. That made the photographers happy, meaning she could quickly slip away.

Marilyn was never Norma Jean in those contexts, and I was never Sammy. It was a case of going into acting mode and putting on a show, and when I stepped out onto the red carpet with Mum that evening, I owned the performance completely and gave them what they needed.

The problems started after the screening, when Mum and I tried to make our way to the restaurant where the première party was being held.

"Where's our car?" Mum asked, glancing around as we stood by the entrance.

"Yeah, where's the driver?" I wondered, searching in vain for the car we had hired for the evening.

Suddenly, a couple of men spotted me and came running. That was like a signal for a load of other young blokes to come charging towards me. And before I had time to work out what was happening, Mum and I were completely surrounded by people, all of them wanting my autograph and trying to grab me—in a nice way, of course. They wanted to touch me.

The situation quickly got worse as more and more people poured in from every direction.

"Dear me," Mum panted with a hint of panic in her voice just as we were both crushed between overexcited fans.

Then we heard a police whistle, and next thing I knew Mum and I had been rescued by a couple of police officers who, with some difficulty, managed to pull us from the crowd and towards a huge police van.

They drove us to the restaurant, Maxim's, which wasn't far away, and as we stumbled inside, it turned out that some of the other guests had seen what had happened. Phil Collins came over and asked, in a concerned voice, whether we were OK. And Steven Spielberg told me that he had been shocked when the chaos broke out.

Not too long after that, something happened that would mark the start of a completely new phase in my life.

I can clearly remember that Mum and I were busy hanging Christmas decorations upstairs in our house when Dad came up and said, "Sammy, some bloke from a record label is coming over tomorrow; he wants to play a song he thinks might be a good fit for you."

"What?" I said, feeling something like an electric shock rush through me.

"Yeah, he says they're looking for the British Madonna."

That night, I couldn't sleep. Of course I had always dreamed of working in music, and when Steven Howard (the man from the record label) came over to play us the demo the next day, it felt like everything had clicked into place for the very first time.

I also liked the fact that Steven used Madonna as a reference. *Like a Virgin* had only recently come out, and Madonna really did personify girl power like no one either before or after her. But above all, I liked the song, and knew it had "hit" written all over it. So when Steven asked, "So, what do you say, would you come and audition?" the answer was obvious.

9

TOUCH ME

It was my first time crowdsurfing, and I
wasn't exactly keen to do it again in a hurry.
Because within the space of a few seconds,
I had a load of thirteen- and fourteen-year-old
hands on my bum, my breasts, everywhere.

The Jive Records office was on Willesden High Road, in the same building as one of their recording studios. There was a second studio on a parallel road, plus another one right next door. Four studios in total, all under the umbrella of Battery Studios. They were home to a whole host of incredible songwriters, producers, and engineers, among them Mark Shreeve. For a significant part of 1985, he had been working on an instrumental record, and Steven Howard, head of A&R at Jive, had taken a liking to one of the tracks that didn't really work on Mark's album. He had then asked Jon Astrop, a songwriter, to come up with a melody and lyrics for it. Jon had been a member of Gang of Four, and coming from that kind of post-punk background, he wasn't all that enthusiastic about the idea. Particularly not since Steven had given him clear instructions on what the song should be about: a young woman on a night out, feeling that sense of energy you only ever experience when everything is new and being tasted for the first time.

In the end, Jon gave in, sat down, and got to work. A few days later, when Steven heard the result, he was over the moon. All that was left was to find an artist. Jon later told me that the first person who came to mind was Sally Ann Triplett, the musical actress, possibly because they were already friends. In any case, Sally actually did sing the song. But neither the lyrics nor the music really suited her, and she was also fully booked up in a West End production. So Jon, Steven, and the others at Jive had to keep looking. Jon even flew over to New York, where no fewer than fifty girls auditioned (that was how much faith Jive had in the song). But no one seemed quite right, and that was when Steven's thoughts turned to me.

I can honestly say that I was massively nervous when I arrived at the studio that morning in early January. There were a load of other girls also waiting to audition, and some of them sang so well that I quickly started to worry. I remember that I was in the studio's kitchen when I heard them over the loudspeakers in the control room. Most of them were completely unknown, but I spotted the actress Leslie Ash waiting on her own, just like I was.

"Hi," she said when she caught sight of me.

"Hi," I said.

Then I went into the toilet to quietly hum my way through the song again. My mouth was dry and my palms were cold and damp. All the same, I'd practiced for several hours every day since Steven came over, and somewhere deep down inside, I knew I could deliver. In fact, by the time my turn finally came around, there wasn't a single hint of doubt left. It was now or never—and without looking any of the other girls in the eye, I went into the booth and gave it everything I had.

The groan in the intro was spontaneous, and I remember that Jon Astrop, who was also the vocal producer, lifted the receiver in the control room and called Steven, who came in to listen. Then one of them pressed the talkback button on the mixing deck so that I could hear them through my headphones, and Steven said, "Could you wait around until all the others have auditioned?"

Once again I had been asked to wait until last, and as the hours passed I was a complete mess of euphoria and expectation. Eventually, I was asked to sing again, and as the last note left my mouth I just knew that it had gone well. Yes, I was inexperienced, but I think that both Jon and Steven could see that I was ready to give them the time and energy that was needed. And just a few days later, I found myself on the phone with Clive Calder, the head of the record label.

"Do you want a singing career?"

"Are you kidding? That's basically what I've been dreaming of my whole life."

"OK, come to my office tomorrow afternoon. Jive wants to offer you a five-album record deal."

The months that followed were magical. Yes, I was working three jobs—model, TV presenter, and singer—and barely had time to sleep or eat. But standing there in the booth at Battery Studios, recording the song that would be my very first solo single—it really was a dream come true. And as time passed, I also relaxed around Jon. He wasn't just a great vocal producer; he also came from the same part of London as me and had the same sense of humor. These were the analog days, when there was no Auto-Tune or any other tricks you could turn to. But I remember that we recorded the song on twelve channels and that Jon mixed them together into one lead vocal track that very same night.

"Sounds good, Jonny boy," I said after listening to it with fresh ears the next morning.

"Yup, we've got it," Jon smiled.

Shortly afterwards, Clive, Steven, and the other record label buys came in to listen, and they were all in agreement that we had a smash hit. They were right. That spring, "Touch Me" would go to number one in no fewer than seventeen countries.

But before the single was released, we needed to record my entire debut album.

Jon contributed another five songs, and since he lived not far from me, he used to pick me up on the way to the studio. He was a real support, someone I could go to for advice on anything to do with the music, but also about the music industry in general.

Aside from Jon, there was a studio manager called Chris Dunn, who took care of the studio and the recording schedule. Then there were Chuck, Paul, and Jerry, fantastic sound technicians all of them.

Robert John "Mutt" Lange, the producer who had worked with bands like Def Leppard and the Cult, was in the studio next door. At that time, he was working with Bryan Adams—not that anyone dared tell me, because they all thought I would storm in and ask for an autograph. Pat McManus from Mama's Boys played guitar on several of my songs. I thought that was cool, since I'd listened to the band a bit. In any case, it didn't take long before I started to appreciate just how much work goes into a record, and I really did put my heart and soul into making sure the songs came out how everyone wanted. While my background as a model had given me opportunities, it also became a heavy burden to carry. To put it bluntly, I wanted to show the world that I wasn't just a model with a record deal. I wanted to prove I was an artist to be reckoned with.

As far as Jive was concerned, everything felt good. They could have chosen a sexy picture of me for the cover of my single or album, or printed one on their merchandise. But they didn't. They launched me as a new pop artist instead, which was precisely what I wanted. Though at the same time, so much felt so unfamiliar. With the journalists from Fleet Street, I knew where I was. They were ordinary, down-to-earth—but the people in the music industry could be snobby and say things like, "Stick to what you're good at." I never really understood that. I mean, I was nineteen, almost twenty, and there was no way I could possibly know exactly what I wanted from life. What nineteen- or twenty-year-old does? Young people try things out as they go along, which is precisely what I was doing. The only difference was that my development was playing out on an open stage, meaning that people noticed every step I took. But just as I hadn't had a grand plan behind sending in a picture to the *Sunday People*'s Face and Shape competition, I had no real long-term plans for my recording career. I lived from one day to the next and grabbed whatever chances I could. I didn't try to present myself as a serious musician, either. Music, for me, was entertainment, something that made people want to dance, sing, and smile.

The first person to play "Touch Me" on British radio was a DJ called Simon Bates, who had a show on BBC Radio 1 at the time. After the track finished, he said, "I can't believe this is Samantha Fox." And then he immediately played it again.

I didn't hear it myself, but people told me about it. I actually heard "Touch Me" on the radio for the first time early one morning in March. Dad had given me a Sony radio when I turned sixteen, and I remember that I woke up to the song playing and initially thought I was dreaming. It's important to remember that a lot of people had slated the song and said things like, "It'll never be a hit." Even when the song really was big, it never made it any higher than Radio 1's C list.

Journalists from *News of the World* had also started phoning Jon practically every day, asking whether it really was me singing on the track.

"Yes, it's Sam singing," he sighed. But they didn't believe him.

One journalist went so far as to offer Jon a whole stack of money to reveal the identity of the real singer. They couldn't believe that a page three girl had sung it all on her own. Eventually, Jon got tired of their nagging and said, "OK, give me the money and I'll tell you who's really singing."

He met the journalist in an industrial area, took the money, and said, "The person singing on Samantha Fox's album is Samantha Fox."

It wasn't long before the song was banned from morning TV and children's programs in Britain, out of fear that it would give the viewers "sexual ideas."

But "Touch Me" didn't need the radio plays. It climbed up the singles charts on its own, largely thanks to practically all of the TV chat shows wanting me to come on as a guest, and to the PA's I was doing all over the UK.

The first was the BBC's Terry Wogan, followed by the *Joan Rivers Show*. If I'm honest, I don't remember much more than that I was insanely nervous, and that it didn't get better when Joan, who had a kind of pushy style, asked whether I was a virgin. I can't remember what I replied, but I later found out that it had been the most viewed BBC2 program ever, with close to eight million viewers.

In my record contract, it said that if the first single reached the top of the Top 40 charts in England, we would record a video. And though I'd been dressed on the covers of both the single and the forthcoming album, the label wanted me to "at least be a little bit sexy" in the video. I remember there was talk about me lying on a bed and singing. In fact, going forward, every single record label representative would suggest that exact scenario. But in my mind, I envisioned more of a Debbie Harry–style video, one in which I was singing on stage with a band. I had some fighting to do—I mean, I was a glamour girl who had recorded a song called "Touch Me." But the record label respected what I said and went along with filming a classic performance video, which would be recorded in a nightclub called Heaven on Villiers Street, London, in mid-March.

It was around this time that Jon Astrop had put together a band who could appear alongside me during TV appearances or PR performances, and the day before we recorded the video, we performed "Touch Me" on *The Wogan Show*, something that resulted in a lot being written about me, above all about my clothes. Before the recording, Mum had ripped a couple of huge holes in my jeans— one on the knee and another right beneath the back pocket. It's something you would see everywhere later, but I was actually the first to do it publicly, and the very next week, pictures were published of Madonna and George Michael both wearing jeans with rips in exactly the same places.

I did, however, steal something completely different from Morten Harket, the singer in A-ha—those rubber bands he wore around his wrists. I thought they looked good, so I quickly got some of my own.

In any case, I mentioned during my appearance on *The Wogan Show* that we needed an audience for the recording of the video. It was true, but I had hardly counted on children and young people from all over England skipping school the next day to catch the first train they could to Charing Cross.

I remember we got started at Heaven early, before the sun had even come up. Film cameras and lighting are pretty expensive to hire, and you pay by the day. That's why the majority of music videos were shot in under twenty-four hours in those days.

I sat to one side having my makeup done while the camera man was busy testing out different angles of the musicians on stage.

The whole club smelled of freshly brewed coffee, and the mood was sleepy. I didn't feel the least bit tired. I was more excited to be making my first real music video. Yes, we had filmed one for SFX, but this was my own, so it felt completely different. The girl doing my makeup seemed to be done, and she asked me to check her work in a huge mirror that had been set up in front of me. Someone had started to let the audience into another part of the club, and in just a few minutes the place was completely packed. I heard someone from the film team shout, "Lock the doors!"

Not long after that, the director's assistant came over to me.

"Ready?"

I nodded and followed her up onto the stage. The audience went completely wild, and I could hear windowpanes breaking out in the entrance. There were so many people that apparently even the locked doors had started to give way. So while I climbed up onto a trapeze and got ready for the first take, the mounted police had to be called, as the club was under the arches at Charing Cross and you couldn't drive right up to the entrance. That whole trapeze scene took a lot of takes to get right. The idea was for me to fly over the audience as I sang into the camera, but since it was incredibly unstable, it was difficult to look relaxed, and I couldn't hold on much longer, so eventually I did fall off it into the crowd. It was my first time crowdsurfing, and I wasn't exactly keen to do it again in a hurry. Because within the space of a second or so, I had a load of thirteen- and fourteen-year-old hands on my bum, my breasts, everywhere. But aside from that incident, everything went well, and I'm still pleased with how it turned out.

A few days later, it was time for my first appearance on the BBC's *Top of the Pops*, the UK's most legendary music program. Just like on other TV shows, we had to mime. The only difference was that the Musicians' Union insisted that we re-record the song in four hours at the BBC's studio. Everyone who performed on *Top of the Pops* had to do the same. That was one of the requirements of being on the show, and it continued until Elton John eventually said, "I'm never re-recording another song. I've spent £120,000 and devoted days and nights to getting it to sound exactly how I want. You can play the record; otherwise you can forget having me on your program."

In any case, our four-hour recording session, which Jon Astrop managed, must have gone well, because after I appeared on the show everything really took off. The single climbed to the third spot in the UK charts. Around the same time, I launched my own clothing line, Sam's Collection, and the pieces started selling in huge numbers via a mail-order catalog. I also opened my own cocktail bar, Sam's, at 669-673 High Road in Tottenham. There was a huge car park outside, with a sign reading "Sam's Parking Place." Two other part-owners looked after the business side of things, but I came up with the concept—hiring twenty or so Samantha Fox look-alikes and naming all the drinks after famous page three models. The idea seemed to work, because the place was packed every evening, and we had a number of well-known Tottenham football players among the regulars. Some people were convinced that one of the girls working there was me (especially after a few drinks), and others hoped to catch a glimpse of me behind the bar. But the truth is that I was hardly ever there. If I had been, I probably would have realized what the two partners were up to.

The girls working in the bar came from different places around the country and they needed somewhere to live, so the partners rented out the rooms on the floor above the bar at exorbitant rates, despite the fact that the rooms were shabby and had no warm water, sometimes not even electricity. I later found out that one of them had invited several girls to have sex with him in exchange for lowering the rent that month. The papers made a huge deal of this, which gave Dad a load to deal with.

Then there was the whole issue of opening hours and alcohol licensing. I don't remember all the details, but on my twentieth birthday, April 15, 1986, I was suddenly summoned to court in Highgate. Mum and Dad were with me, and I remember I had my hair up and that I was wearing a jacket that covered most of my bust. I also remember that Dad had gone over what I needed to say again and again.

But I was still incredibly nervous, which wasn't helped by coming face to face with the press, who were watching the entire thing. Even if I had nothing to do with the bar in practical terms, I still owned 50 percent of the business, and I almost felt like a criminal. I mean, it was a real courtroom, something I'd only ever seen on TV before, and when my barrister opened with the simple question "What are the opening hours at Sam's Bar?" I suddenly had a complete blackout.

I swallowed and stuttered, "Weekdays, eleven to twelve thirty . . . uh . . . Oh, God, I can't remember the hours . . . Sundays ten thirty to two. No . . . twelve to two . . ."

Simply put, the situation got to me so much that my entire mind went blank.

Then the judge said that, as the license holder, I was expected to know when the bar was open, and that I should have an overview of the business.

I looked at Dad, who seemed like he was forcing himself to stay calm. Then I swallowed again before I assured the judge that of course I was in control of the bar; I just couldn't remember the opening hours at that particular moment. Obviously, I thought it was all over, but somehow, miraculously (don't ask me how), everything sorted itself out and we were allowed to keep the place open as usual.

10

AN EVENING
WITH QUEEN

*"Sam, they haven't got any knickers on." I looked
down and saw their green-dyed pubic hair and thought,
"This is going to be a wild party."*

"Touch Me" had topped the single charts across Europe, and my debut album had just begun to climb the album charts, too. But that didn't mean that people in the music industry accepted me for it. It was like I wasn't in their clique. In their eyes, I was just a page three girl who'd gotten lucky with a hit. But then, one evening in spring 1986, something happened that would change everything.

I'd been invited to a party organized by Queen, and my friend Suzanne Dando and I had decided we would go. Before I had my breakthrough as an artist, I hung out almost exclusively with other models. In the long run, it was actually pretty boring, because they only ever talked about modeling and other superficial things. But Suzanne and I could talk about anything, and we went out together quite a lot during that time. On that particular night, we had a few drinks at my bar and then took a taxi to Kensington Gardens, where the party was being held.

The weather was mild and comfortable like it sometimes is in London in spring, and we were both slightly tipsy and feeling great.

The place was called the Roof Gardens, in Kensington, and was at the very top of the building. I'll never forget the moment we stepped into the lift and were welcomed by a couple of girls who were painted from head to toe.

Suzanne leaned over and whispered, "Sam, they haven't got any knickers on." I looked down and saw their green-dyed pubic hair and thought to myself, *This is going to be a wild party.*

Not long afterwards, when we made it up to the club, we were greeted by dwarves carrying trays of drinks. I'd never seen anything like it, and we still hadn't even made it into the actual party. Music was blaring from the speakers, the air was heavy and scented, and everyone who was anyone was there—Kim Wilde, Frankie Goes to Hollywood, Duran Duran, to name just a few.

The Roof Gardens isn't a big place, and we quickly reached the small stage that had been built along one wall. Suddenly, we saw Freddie Mercury, Brian May, and a couple of others jump up and start jamming. A moment later, Gary Glitter stepped onto the stage and played his seventies hit "Do You Wanna Touch Me (Oh Yeah)." That was roughly when Freddie caught sight of me and pulled me up onto the stage.

I was completely overwhelmed by a surreal feeling.

"Which songs do you know?" he shouted.

"'Touch Me,'" I stammered.

Freddie laughed.

"I mean cover songs."

"'Tutti Frutti!'"

Not long after that, we sang it together. Then Brian May started on one of his signature long guitar solos, and Freddie and I danced. Though maybe "danced" is the wrong word. He threw me around like a rag doll, swinging his hips for all he was worth, and I laughed so hard I had a coughing fit.

Everyone got pretty drunk that night, and I woke the next day to huge pictures of me and Freddie in the papers. I can clearly remember how much it meant to me back then. Partly because *he* had chosen to

Two years old,
with Mum.

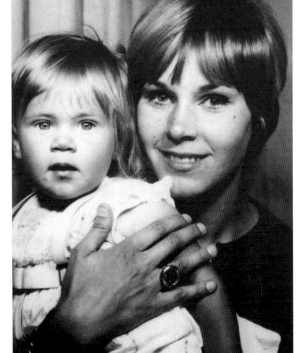

One year old.

Two years old,
with Dad.

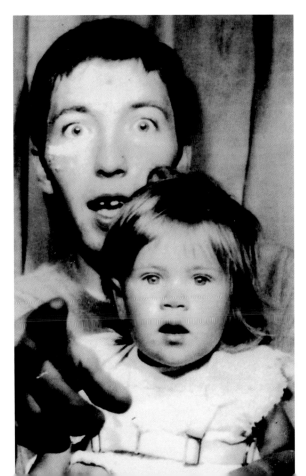

My grandmother, *middle*, getting married for the second time, to her Harry. I'm holding Mum's hand and wearing my calipers and built-up shoe. Dad is in one of his many fashionable suits. Harry's brother and sister-in-law are at the side.

Vanessa, *right*, at her confirmation.

With Dad in Cornwall during a car holiday the family went on in summer 1977. We drove through places like Devon in our Volkswagen Beetle.

The "Another Woman" video shoot at Finchley Lido, where I used to go swimming with Mum as a child. Mum is my stylist here.

I was over the moon with the car Peter Foster gave me for Christmas 1986. But I didn't have a driving license, so all I could do was drive it up and down the street outside our house. Dad is admiring it here.

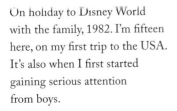

On holiday to Disney World with the family, 1982. I'm fifteen here, on my first trip to the USA. It's also when I first started gaining serious attention from boys.

One of my early page three shots. (Photo by Beverly Goodway)

With Smokey Robinson in Montreux, 1988. He asked me to wear his jacket so he could take my scent back to the USA with him. That evening, I also met Chrissie Hynde and Whitney Houston.

With Elvis Costello from the first time I performed "Touch Me" on TV. It was on Terry Wogan's chat show—the same day my aunt Maureen passed away.

With Joey Tempest at the *Okej* magazine offices in Stockholm, 1987. I'm presenting Europe with a gold record for their album *The Final Countdown*.

With the Pet Shop Boys, Neil Tennant, *right,* and Chris Lowe, *left,* at the recording of *Top of the Pops*, 1987.

Swinging out over the audience during the recording of the video for "Touch Me" at the Heaven nightclub, 1986.

In the dressing room at the Hippodrome, 1986, ahead of my first live performance of "Touch Me" during the World Disco Dancing Championship. Bros were my support act.

With Chrissie on holiday in Cancún, roughly one year after we first met.

With my matador boyfriend, Rafi, at a restaurant in Marbella, 1991.

Lemmy and me backstage at the Royal Festival Hall, ahead of a Hawkwind reunion gig, where I was asked to sing their "Master of the Universe." It was a complete mess up onstage; the band members were high as kites, their eyes wide, and I thought, "Jesus, am I really going to sing with these guys?"

Paul and me.

With Paul on the bus from Schipol airport in Amsterdam, where KISS were playing a gig with Van Halen. Prior to this, we had been at the Monsters of Rock festival in Donington. It was 1988.

My beloved
cat Talulah.

With Jonathan
King at my twentieth
birthday party
at Stringfellows
in London.

sing with *me*, and partly because people from the music industry had finally realized that I really could sing. From then on, whenever I bumped into those eighties stars in TV studios or elsewhere, they treated me with a completely different quality of respect.

It wasn't long after all of this happened that Freddie withdrew from the world. I often used to go to a club called Browns, where I would sometimes see Brian May's girlfriend, Anita Dobson, who starred in the BBC's *Eastenders* at the time. I asked her how Freddie was doing. I didn't know he was sick back then, but she told me that he was staying away from everyone and everything. On one occasion, she told me that he had said hello, but when I asked whether I could go to see him, she said, "Sam, he doesn't want to see anyone."

The reviews of my debut album weren't uniformly positive. Or maybe you could summarize it like this: the music critics in the UK virtually never gave good reviews to anyone who looked good, but the pop stars who looked like scruffy students, they got top marks.

That said, the public was on my side from the very beginning, and when I went to HMV to sign copies of the album, the queue stretched right along Oxford Street. Thousands of people turned up, and I was signing my name nonstop for five hours. When men asked for autographs, they sometimes wanted me to put a kiss after my name, which I usually did. But some went further and wanted me to write things like, "Thanks for last night." There was no end to my creativity when it came to greetings, but a kiss was as suggestive as I was willing to get.

When I went on a signing tour in Germany not long afterwards, I discovered something else that happened when I met male fans. I don't remember the exact location, but I was in a huge shopping center and Dad was with me. There were more people than we had expected, so I was put on a little stage in the middle of the shopping center rather than in the record store itself. I was meant to sit at a table on the stage, and the security guards tried to get people to form an orderly queue, which soon proved impossible—they were crowding forward from every direction. The guards did what they could to push back anyone who got too close, and they occasionally had to carry men away. When that happened, I noticed that the men had erections!

I was completely shocked and looked at Dad, who had seen it too. There was a certain hint of stress in his eyes when he mumbled, "The blood's gone to their heads."

After that, I saw many erections when I was out and about with work, for the simple reason that I paid more attention to it.

Another signing that sticks in my mind was at the Allders department store in Basildon, back in England. The entire shop was a throng of men, and two fights broke out in the crowd. All I could hear were voices shouting, "Samantha, Samantha, Sammeee, please, over here . . . Whatta little doll, give us a kiss . . . Shake my hand . . . Mine too, please . . . Oh, Christ, I've just touched her . . ." followed by a female voice over the tannoy:

"Calm down, calm down. Samantha Fox will be here for an hour, and you'll all get a signed picture."

Again I was shown to a table on a small stage, and Dad, who was almost always with me, whispered in my ear, "Just your signature now, Sammy. No personal greetings, otherwise we'll be here forever."

Most things in my life really were hysterical around that point in time. The daily papers wrote about me practically every day, and even something as trivial as a trip to the hairdresser's could result in a headline. I remember one big article, which appeared in the *Sun* at some point during spring 1986, that was about girls who looked like me. The headline was: "Meet Four Foxy Ladies Who Keep Getting Mistaken for Samantha Fox."

Another tabloid published an article about a mother who had baked a birthday cake in the shape of my breasts for her twelve-year-old son. Yet another featured an article about a young artist who painted pictures of me. Another paper wrote about a kid in his late teens who had a motorbike accident. When he woke up in hospital and his dad asked whether there was anything he wanted, he said, "Samantha Fox," so his dad went out to buy a life-sized poster of me. But the craziest story of all, published in the *Sun*, had to be the one about Chris Tiney, a twenty-five-year-old who lived with his wife, and she accepted that he had pictures of me all over the house. According to the article, he had even taken down two pictures of his wife to replace them with pictures of me. But when he tried to swap their wedding picture in their bedroom, she finally put her foot down.

In teenage magazines around this time, girls could vote on whether they would rather be me or Madonna. I won every time. There were telephone lines you could call up just to listen to my voice, and a game where you could play strip poker with me was launched on the Commodore 64. It actually became a massive hit in several countries, thanks largely to its release coinciding with my breakthrough with "Touch Me."

But even though it was great that everything was going well and that I—a working-class girl from Morgan Mansions—was now more famous than Margaret Thatcher, it was getting really tough not to be able to go outside. Or to Arsenal's home games, like I'd always done with Dad. There was no point in even thinking about being in the stands with fifty thousand blokes. Even the most ordinary of activities started to feel exhausting: going for a walk, doing the food shopping. There were always people coming up to me, wanting to talk or to get an autograph.

I always wore sunglasses and sportswear, and quite often went without makeup. In other words, I tried to make myself as invisible as I could. But people still recognized me, which sometimes felt incredibly claustrophobic. I quickly learned that if I ignored the staring, it only got worse. The best thing I could do was show them I had seen them. Then, it was like they came to their senses and looked away. Some men still came over, looking completely terrified even to talk to me, and others shouted clichés like, "So it *is* you; I didn't recognize you with your clothes on."

On one occasion, I even bumped into a man who had my name tattooed across his forehead. It was insane, of course—and back then, I had no idea how many similar, and sometimes even much worse, things I would see during the years that followed.

In the midst of all this chaos, news reached me that the naked pictures taken in Antigua had now turned up in American porn mags that had been smuggled into Britain and sold for crazy amounts of money. In these magazines, which I think were called *Live* and *High Society*, they called me Suzanna. The images had captions like, "FUCK ME!' Screams Suzanna"—continuing in that vein for page after page. Aside from the fact I was only seventeen in those pictures (which was against the law; girls in that kind of magazine had to be at least eighteen), the whole thing obviously felt incredibly tasteless.

In 1986, I was still under contract with the *Sun*, so whenever I wasn't promoting my new record I was modeling in a photography studio somewhere. For those jobs, which took an hour and a half, I never got paid more than fifty pounds. The big money came from the jobs on the side. I was paid for interviews, and whenever I did a photo shoot for an American magazine, I remember earning around ten thousand pounds per job. But I still used to buy all my makeup and underwear from Marks and Sparks. Maybe it was down to my working-class roots, but I just didn't think it was worth spending much on.

With time, I also learned to argue back. I remember, for example, getting changed ahead of a photo shoot and being pretty unhappy with the underwear I was trying on. It had cost me six hundred pounds, which was a huge amount for underwear back then, so it annoyed me that it didn't sit right. But the photographer stuck his head around the curtain and said, "You don't need to worry; your breasts really are perfect. They're the reason everyone loves you."

"No, they're not at all," I replied. "People look at my pretty, smiling face in the morning and then work their way down."

But yes, I was still only twenty, and sometimes all the pressure could be a lot to cope with. Some days, I lost all my self-confidence, broke down, and cried. And I could be very critical of my body. It was as though I didn't see it as part of me, more as a tool for my work, something I earned money from. It was also boring to constantly be asked about my breasts. I mean, how long can a person talk about a pair of breasts? And the papers always wanted me to look the same in their pictures, too—same hair, same pose, same type of makeup. They wanted people to immediately realize that it was Samantha Fox when they turned the page. I remember I tried wearing my hair in a different style once, but the photographer just turned around and said, "Jesus Christ, you're not doing *Vogue* or *Cosmopolitan*, darling."

I also remember often being asked, for the sake of equality, whether I thought they should have a spread of page three boys, too. But I replied that I didn't think men looked all that nice when they were naked. That kind of statement wasn't always well received in all quarters, and aside from the music critics, it was probably the feminists who least appreciated what I was doing. I remember, for example, that a female British politician attacked me and the other page three girls, claiming that our glamour shots were the main cause of a rise in the number of rapes in Britain. It was insane, of course. But above all, that kind of argument involved a tired double standard. I mean, someone like Glenda Jackson, a popular actress at the time, could be topless in a film and it would be seen as art.

Anyway, now that I'd had my first hit, I wanted to get out there on tour and show people what I was made of. But Dad didn't understand. He said we could earn more money by sending me to do various playback gigs or PAs around Europe. He really did only ever think about the money. And since he was the way he was, and I respected him, I never dared argue. But honestly, I would have happily earned considerably less money and found a band that could gig with me. As things stood, I would perform "Touch Me," then another song, and then "Touch Me" again—all as singback. It felt cheap, and I hated it.

Dad couldn't understand why it was so important for me to be a real artist. It wasn't until I'd really broken through in the US that he finally understood the point of touring. But before that, I managed to fall head over heels for an incredibly charismatic man from Down Under.

11

PETER FOSTER

*[Peter had] an energy like no one I'd ever met, either
before or after. His entire being was enthusiastic. He
was one of those people who could make almost anything
feel like a party, who could make practically anything he
turned his hand to a success.*

"Sammy, come and say hello!"

It must have been early in the morning, because I was still in bed
when I heard Dad shout. My first thought was that a journalist
must have come over, someone I'd arranged an interview with and
then forgotten. But after I pulled on a pair of jeans and a baggy
eighties muscle shirt and rushed downstairs, I quickly realized that
wasn't the case. Sitting at the kitchen table opposite Dad was a man
in his mid-twenties, with dark, wavy hair. The minute he saw me,
he got up and introduced himself as Peter.

"Sam," I smiled, stifling a yawn.

"Just woke up?"

I nodded and realized that I hadn't put on any makeup or brushed
my hair.

"The contract's ready to sign," Dad said, nodding to a stack of
papers on the table. Right then, I remembered that he had been
talking about a man from Australia who wanted to use me in the
advertising campaign for his weight-loss tea. This had to be him.

I went over to the table and signed the papers. That was how it worked in our family. If Dad told me to sign something, I signed it. And if I wanted to buy anything, I had to ask him for money. It wasn't something I even thought about, maybe because I was just so used to it. Dad had always taken care of all of Mum's money and paperwork, too.

Peter took his copies of the contract and thanked us both. Before he left, we looked at one another properly for the first time. I remember that his eyes lingered for a little too long. There was an instant attraction. He said later that he loved my naturalness with no makeup and my sportswear.

A few weeks later, we had invited a few friends and business contacts over to the house, and for some reason I found myself thinking of Peter. I called him and asked if he wanted to come, too. He did, and I think that was the evening I realized there was something special about him. Not least as the clock was approaching midnight and I went over to ask if he wanted to dance. He was talking to a couple of other guests at the time—I've forgotten who—but I can clearly remember that he looked up at me and said, with some kind of superior expression on his face, "No."

I raised my eyebrow. "What do you mean?"

Peter grinned, and then he said, "I read an article in the paper about the life of Samantha Fox. There was a quote in it, saying you could get any man you wanted. This is one you're not going to get."

No one had ever said anything like that to me before, and I remember turning to the people he had been talking to and playing indignant: "I can't believe it. I'm Samantha Fox and he won't dance with me."

I moved on and mingled with the others, but I didn't give up the idea of that dance, and at about five in the morning we really did dance with one another. All the other guests had left by that point, and before Peter got into a taxi, I said, "Perhaps we should have dinner sometime."

"Well," he said, "how about tomorrow night?"

Peter really did have an energy like no one I'd ever met, either before or after. His entire being was enthusiastic. He was one of those people who could make almost anything feel like a party, who could make practically anything he turned his hand to a success.

But what I didn't know was that Peter was a criminal and that he had begun his career when he was just seventeen, working as a boxing promoter in Australia. He had, among other things, arranged a fight between the British light heavyweight boxer Bunny Johnson and a local fighter called Tony Mundine. Ahead of the fight, Peter had taken out an insurance policy that would pay forty thousand pounds if it was canceled because someone got injured. Oddly enough, Bunny managed to trap his hand in a car door two days before the fight and had to pull out. The insurance company saw through the scam, of course, and Peter found himself thrown into a drawn-out legal battle. Eventually, with Bunny, he was fined seventy-five thousand pounds in damages and a hundred thousand in legal costs.

It was around then that Peter came up with the idea of getting involved in health foods and miracle cures. This was where his weight-loss tea, Bai Lin Tea, came into the picture. Peter had hired the swimmer Dawn Fraser, and a model called Lyn Barron, who was married to *Blue Lagoon* star Christopher Atkins, to be ambassadors for the product in Australia. But the Australian consumer standards agency quickly determined that Lyn had been in good shape even before the drink was launched on the market. Plus, Peter had gone on record as saying that the drink had helped Lester Piggott, the jockey, to win the Australian Oaks, which led to a number of complaints.

But Peter's departure for England, where he was now planning to market his Bai Lin Tea with me by his side, was no PR bluff; he simply had not bothered to send the tea to the hundreds of thousands of people who had bought it. Even now, I have no idea why. Peter was so gifted that there was no need for him to trick people. He would have been successful anyway. Plus, there was nothing wrong with the tea itself. It was a green tea, which has since been shown to have health benefits.

In any case, the tea had made Peter rich, and not long after we started dating, he started showering me with presents. If we walked past a shop window and I saw something I liked, for example, he would head straight inside and buy it. He sent me telegrams when I was away with work, and I would often come back to my hotel room to find a bottle of champagne and a bowl of fresh strawberries. Peter was just incredibly romantic, and in the autumn of 1986 he took me to Kenya on what would be an eventful safari.

I remember that we flew first class to Nairobi and that from there we chartered a private plane to Masai Mara. To avoid being followed by the press, the reservations at each of the hotels were made under "Mr. and Mrs. Foster," but there was still a journalist and a photographer from the *Sun* waiting for us when we landed.

Both Peter and I were tired from the journey, and realizing that we would have to negotiate with them hardly made us feel any better. In the end, we managed to come to a deal that would allow them to take pictures during our first day if they agreed to leave us in peace afterwards.

Roughly at the same time this was happening, children suddenly came running towards us from all directions. They were begging, but I didn't have anything to give them—nothing other than cigarettes. So, in the end, I gave them a couple of packets, thinking that they could give them to their parents. The only issue was that this happened just as the *Sun* was wanting to take pictures of me with them, and a couple of the kids decided to open the packets and shove the cigarettes into their mouths. When the article was published, of course, there was a huge fuss. Not just because the children in the pictures had cigarettes in their mouths, but also because of the disgusting headline: "Sam Fox Teaches the African Children to Smoke."

We checked into our hotel, the Tree Tops, the same hotel where the Queen had been staying when she heard that her father, George VI, had died in 1952. A few hours later, we headed off on our first day trip to the Masai Mara itself.

The Maasai people lived in mud huts with thatched roofs, and all of the women were bare-breasted. They started dancing as soon as they spotted us, and I heard the photographer whisper to Peter, "It would be amazing to get a picture of Sam topless next to those Maasai women."

I felt a bit uncomfortable, but Peter promised he would ask the tribal chief. Next thing I knew, we were inside one of the huts, since that's where the photographer next to me wanted us. It turned out she was the wife of the tribal chief. Peter was asking a young, bare-breasted woman, through an interpreter, whether she would sit down next to me. Peter handed fifty pounds to the chief, who pulled up a chair and told Peter to sit down and relax.

The woman, who had now come over, looked at me and then patted the ground beside her. I was at a complete loss. Suddenly, Peter started to laugh and said, "I think they want me to film while you have sex with her!"

I looked over to the young woman, who was still smiling invitingly. Then I quickly got up and ran out.

The next incident took place a few days later, once we had escaped the journalist and photographer from the *Sun* and traveled to the Masai Mara Game Reserve to stay in a luxury resort made up of a number of tents. To get there, you had to wade across a river that was full of hippos. They can be incredibly aggressive, and I voiced my concerns to Peter.

"I don't have a good feeling about crossing here, hon. We should call for help."

But Peter just laughed and said, "Come on, they're really cute."

As luck would have it, they left us in peace. But I did get bitten by an insect, which made one of my eyes swell up. It stayed like that the whole week we were there. Still, I remember Peter constantly saying, "You're so beautiful . . . You really are."

The resort really did have all the same facilities and mod cons as any other luxury hotel, so after we had been shown to our tent, we went to the bar to calm ourselves down. Or rather, to calm me down. In any case, I ordered a Baileys and Peter chose a Tia Maria. But before we even had time to take a sip, an older white gentleman came out from one of the other tents and sat down at the table next to ours.

"Did you hear that a herd of elephants came charging straight through here a few years ago?"

Both Peter and I stared at him.

"My God!" I said. "What happened to the guests?"

"They died."

"They died?"

"Oh yes," the man chuckled. "They all died!"

The hotel guard was standing a bit away from us. He was wearing nothing but a loincloth, and the only weapon I could see was a spear that he was leaning against. I mean, how was he meant to use that to protect us if a herd of elephants came charging in? Or what about a couple of hungry lions? Don't get me wrong, I love animals, but I don't want to be trampled to death or eaten by one. Peter didn't, either, so when we got back to our tent later that night and heard growling sounds from somewhere nearby, neither of us could sleep. It didn't get any better the next day—or rather the next evening—either.

There was only one shower in our tent, so once Peter was finished he told me to meet him in the bar when I was ready. And then he left.

When you're in the wilderness, in that tropical heat, there's nothing better than taking a shower, and I stood beneath the running water for quite some time. But just as I began to lather myself up, I heard some kind of grunting sound on the other side of the tent wall. I turned off the water and looked down, and through the eye that wasn't swollen shut, I saw a gigantic warthog. I froze to the spot, especially since the wall of the tent had started to move by my feet. Next thing I knew, a pair of huge tusks had appeared under the tent, and the warthog was using its tusks to pull it up. The guard was standing only a few yards away, and I waved for him to come over. But since I was naked, he started running in the opposite direction. He was probably worried about being accused of sexual harassment or something, but it meant I was completely alone with the warthog, so I kept flicking it with my towel. I took a few quick breaths and then shouted as loudly as I could, "Peeeeeeter!" But he probably thought I'd just found a new insect bite or something, and stayed where he was.

After what felt like an eternity, when the warthog finally disappeared, I crept cautiously out of the tent and headed to the bar. I found Peter sitting with the same old gentleman as before, and when I told them what had happened, the man just chuckled, "They love soap! Oh, yes, they love soap!"

The incidents came one after another, but I still have to say that it was one of the best holidays I've ever been on. Plus, coming home would actually prove much more dangerous. Dad came to pick us up from Heathrow, and the first thing he did was drive straight into the back of a car that had braked suddenly in front of us. Somehow, it felt ironic. I mean, we had spent almost two weeks in the wilderness, surrounded by wild animals, and now our lives were being put at risk by a terrible middle-aged driver.

A few weeks later, I was on the road again—to Australia this time, to promote my album. Both Dad and Peter came with me, and the entire airport was full of fans and journalists when we landed. That was probably the first time I really started to suspect that things weren't quite as they should be with Peter and his business, though I didn't want to admit it to myself; my feelings for him were just too strong.

Now, looking back, I think it's fair to say that Peter is the only man I ever truly loved. Now I was arriving with him in his homeland to find that all kinds of things were being written about him in the Australian papers—and when I appeared on a talk show hosted by a man called Terry Willasee on our first day in Sydney, Peter was all they wanted to know about. Eventually, it got to me, and I said, "Listen, I haven't come all the way from England to talk about my boyfriend!"

I stood up, forgetting that I needed to take off my mic. I got stuck and started waving my hands to try to get loose. The program was being broadcast live, and lots of people thought I was giving the host the finger, but I really wasn't. I just thought that he was shameless and did everything I could to get the mic off me so that I could leave.

Something else that gave me misgivings as far as Peter was concerned came a few days later, when we went to the Gold Coast, near Brisbane. He wanted to show me and Dad where he lived. I remember jumping when I saw the bullet holes in the front door, and Peter's explanation didn't exactly make me any calmer.

"Some people heard I had a load of money at home, so they forced their way in, tied my then girlfriend to a chair in the kitchen, and hit me with their guns to try to make me tell them where the money was."

Just then, I realized Dad looked concerned, too.

With time, Peter started to get more and more jealous. He also continued to spoil me with expensive presents. When I woke up one morning in December, for example, there was a brand-new red Mercedes 380 SL parked outside my window, with a huge red bow around it. Peter came up with more business ideas, too, and among them, he financed and launched my and Mum's own beauty line, called Jumelle.

All the same, I was starting to feel uneasy about his controlling side. Dad tried to control me, too, particularly when he could see Peter doing the same, and by the time I got home from Australia they really had grown to hate one another. Peter said that Dad shouldn't be my manager. He warned me about him, not just once but several times, and now, with hindsight, I can see that I should have listened to him. But back then, I didn't know whether I could trust Peter. Particularly considering everything the papers wrote about him.

In October that year, "Touch Me" had started getting quite a few plays in the US, and as a result of that I was offered work as a VJ with MTV in New York. A few weeks later, I was on a plane across the Atlantic, with plans to spend the next twenty-five days doing PR for the single and presenting videos on the TV channel that was about to take over the world. My slot was in the morning, just as people were getting ready for work. But most of my time was still spent on traditional PR work.

Aside from signing copies of the single in record shops in New York and a show at a club in Manhattan, I had to find time to fly to LA to appear on the American equivalent of *Top of the Pops*. I also needed to make it to Houston and Canada for a number of interviews. On top of all this, *Playboy* had offered me a hundred thousand pounds for a topless shoot, but I felt that from a tactical point of view, it was wrong. In the US and throughout the rest of the world, I wanted the music to speak for itself.

Looking back, the decision seems sensible, because while I was in the US "Touch Me" reached the top five on the *Billboard* charts, and over twenty-five thousand copies of a special edition of the single were sold, in only eighteen hours, at a couple of signings in New York.

Despite all that, I still felt lonely whenever I went back to my hotel room at night. I didn't have Mum, Dad, or Peter with me, and I remember spending a fortune on phone calls. There was no Internet then, so, being alone in New York City, I felt a bit cut off from homely things. That feeling of longing for someone really was frustrating. Plus, the working tempo was incredibly high. There was constantly a limo waiting outside, and I had so many interviews booked that sometimes I didn't even have time to eat.

For quite a long time, I had been looking for a new home for myself and my family. I was tired of everyone knowing where I lived. From early in the morning until late in the evening, and sometimes even throughout the night, there were people outside the house, just waiting to catch a glimpse of me or get my autograph. And it wasn't just Londoners or Brits; they now came from all over the world. Not even the postman could resist knocking on our door to ask for my autograph late one day. That's why, right after I got home from the US, it felt great to buy a pink, 150-year-old cottage in Hertfordshire, complete with huge, parklike garden.

The house was completely detached, not overlooked at all, and I had also taken the opportunity to buy and install a studio. The only problem was that when we came to move in, the girlfriend of the man who had sold us the house refused to move out, claiming he had promised her a percentage of the money from the sale. Obviously, that had nothing to do with me, but the papers made a big deal of it and the girl sold them pictures of my new home, meaning everyone knew where I lived once again.

On December 1, I flew to Japan for the first time. My debut single was doing well over there, and now the Japanese fans wanted to know more about the person behind the track. Mum came with me, and it was a really stressful trip. Back then, flying over Russia (the Soviet Union at the time) was prohibited, so we had to fly to Tokyo via Anchorage in Alaska, meaning the entire journey took over twenty hours.

We'd heard that according to Japanese custom, we would receive small gifts when we arrived, and that we would need to have something to give in exchange. I remember that I took some earrings (which were always huge and over-the-top back then) and some bangles, and when I handed them over to the Japanese PR girls who came to meet us at the airport, they reacted like I'd just given them a million pounds.

We were only going to be in Tokyo for three days, so the minute I got into the car that would take us into town, I was handed the schedule of everything I needed to fit in. It was around ten thirty at night, and the first interview was scheduled for seven thirty the following morning. The next one was at eight, and the day would continue like that, without a break for lunch or dinner.

To western ears, Japanese people have unusual names, but as it happened, the record label boss was called Ken. So whenever we had any questions, it was Ken we turned to—since his was the only name we actually managed to remember. Two o'clock came and went and I was beyond hungry, so I said, "Ken, do you think you could order us some food?"

Ken nodded and said something to his assistant in Japanese, and I continued with my umpteenth interview in a row. A few minutes later, a huge plate of raw fish arrived. Back then, you couldn't get either sushi or sashimi in England, and I'd never even heard of it. And yes, it looked pretty, but there was basically no way I would be able to eat it right there and then, so I asked for a Big Mac instead— which caused a great deal of laughter and chatter among the Japanese people. They must have thought I was crazy.

Japanese record labels always want their own album covers, and Avex Trax, my label, was no different. So as soon as I wolfed down my hamburger, we headed to a photo studio for an album cover shoot.

They had translated all the song lyrics from English to Japanese and printed them inside the cover, and at some point a Japanese fan explained to me that it made the texts completely different.

I would make more trips to Japan in the years to come, among them for performances in Nagoya, Osaka, and Tokyo, and I was always surprised by how reserved the Japanese were. Whenever you hugged them, they went completely stiff. Plus, the audiences always stayed in their seats during the show. On one occasion, I felt like I just had to get them up, and after I finished a song I went behind the curtain. I cautiously peered out and jokingly shouted, "If you don't stand up I'll go back to London!" Sadly, it didn't work, because they didn't understand a word of English. But at another show, I finally got them to stand. I thanked them and said they could sit down again, but that just made them applaud even more.

12

NOTHING'S GONNA STOP ME NOW

"Could I please ask you to wear my jacket for just a little while? I want it to smell like you when I take it back to America."

"Sam, do you like Bon Jovi?"

The question came from one of the producers at MTV. It was spring 1987, and I was in New York almost constantly. MTV wanted me to continue presenting videos for them, plus they backed all my single releases.

"Uh . . . sure," I replied honestly. I mean, who didn't like Bon Jovi back then? The band had had a mega hit with "Livin' on a Prayer" a year or so earlier, and Jon Bon Jovi himself was every girl's dream.

"Good, because we want to send you to Jamaica with them next week."

The setup was completely insane. For an entire weekend, the band and I would party and play up for the cameras at a hotel called, fittingly enough, Hedonism, just outside the small beach resort of Negril. It was like some kind of early reality show.

I took Dad with me—or maybe he just decided he was coming along—and when we arrived at the hotel, we could barely believe our eyes.

On the beach just outside, there were naked people everywhere. It turned out there was a nudist beach next to our hotel's private beach, and we barely had time to put down our bags before Dad said, "Uh, hmm . . . I think I'm going for a little walk along the beach . . . I need some fresh air . . ."

And with that, he disappeared.

I soon realized that the entire hotel was practically made for partying. They played loud reggae all day long and the drinks at the bar were free. There were probably a hundred or so people involved in the TV production in one way or another, and I wouldn't be lying if I said that the vast majority were completely wasted almost the entire time we were there.

The plan was for me and the boys from Bon Jovi to present new music videos at various intervals while we hung out by the pool, on the beach, at the bar, etc. It goes without saying that things occasionally got a little out of hand. But it made good TV, especially when the boys started talking with Jamaican accents. There was lots of "No proooblem man," and "Relaaaax maan."

I was still with Peter at the time, and since I—if I'm completely honest—had a massive crush on Jon, I found the whole thing a bit frustrating. Plus, Jon had brought his girlfriend with him, a girl called Dorothea who shot me hostile looks as she slowly and carefully rubbed tanning oil into his back.

But Jon often stole glances at me, particularly when we were playing beach volleyball. I was on the pill at the time, and all the estrogen made my breasts practically twice their usual size. Jumping around after the ball in a bikini, I could really feel his eyes on me.

One person who hadn't brought his girlfriend was the guitarist, Richie Sambora. He was the naughty boy in the band, and as we were getting ready to go sailing on a huge catamaran called Great

Eagle one day, he turned up dragging a huge amount of beer behind him.

"We've already loaded plenty of beer and spirits, Richie," the producer shouted over to him.

"I know," Richie grinned, dumping his beer into the boat anyway.

After the sailing trip, everyone felt pretty merry, but Richie wasn't done. He said he knew a great place we could go that evening, Jenny's Cake House.

"What kind of place is it?" I asked.

"Come with me and you'll find out," he said with a wink.

I was still pretty naive at the time and really did think we were going to some kind of nice café. I felt pretty disappointed later that evening when I saw the huge blue and white shack in the sunset.

"Is this it?" I asked Richie, who was walking ahead of me.

"Yeah, come on!" he said, waving for Dad and me to follow him.

The décor inside was simple, to say the least, but the mood was charged, and we were soon sitting down, each with a cup of mushroom tea. The wrinkled old woman who owned the place and served us the tea also offered us, with a toothless grin, huge hash brownies she had baked herself.

Other than a couple of joints I had smoked during my teens, I didn't have much experience of drugs, and after drinking half a cup of that tea and almost immediately feeling high, I decided not to drink any more. I also said a polite no to the hash brownie.

The boys from Bon Jovi weren't anywhere near as cautious, particularly not Richie. He quickly downed two cups of mushroom tea and then climbed up onto the table.

"I'm a big bird!" he shouted.

And with that, he started jumping from table to table, flapping his arms and hooting loudly.

Dad, who was sitting next to the keyboard player, David Bryan, looked up at Richie, who was still screeching and flapping around, and then down at his empty cup. He said, "What is this crap? I don't feel a thing."

He waved to the old woman and asked her to refill his cup. He emptied it in one gulp and waited.

"Still don't feel anything," he said after a while, waving his hand in the air impatiently.

Jon looked over to Dad and said, "Be careful, Pat. Be careful."

"Ah, nothing's happening," Dad said as the woman refilled his cup to the brim.

I saw Jon and Tico Torres, the drummer, exchange glances over the table.

Dad had drunk four cups of the mushroom tea, and it was suddenly as though someone had hit him over the head with a huge wooden stick. One minute he was sitting there, talking to David like normal, but two seconds later when I glanced in his direction, he was completely wasted, and I mean *completely wasted*. He was cross-eyed and could barely even keep himself upright.

I realized I needed to get him back to the hotel, so I asked David and Jon to help him up from his seat and then I supported him as he staggered out of Jenny's Cake House with his arm around my neck.

It was a real struggle getting him all the way back to the hotel, and when we finally made it to the lobby, it was full of drunk people in huge white sheets. They were American teenagers having a toga party, but Dad had started to hallucinate by that point, and he seriously thought they were ghosts.

"Oh no, oh no!!" he wailed, waving his arms so wildly that I thought he was about to topple over.

He was completely paranoid, and I had a tough job getting him into the lift so we could go upstairs. Eventually, I managed to get him into bed. Though sadly that didn't help much.

"AHHH!!!" he shouted, pointing wide-eyed at something only he could see.

"Easy, Dad. Easy," I tried, but the minute I attempted to get up from the bed he grabbed my arm as though he was about to drown.

"Don't leave me! Don't leave me!" he shouted, his face pale and clammy and with so much fear in his eyes it was almost scary.

I had never seen my dad like that before. He was someone who was always in control of himself, and ideally also of his environment. But now he was suddenly exposed to all these figments of his imagination and completely powerless to get rid of them.

I sat by his side all night, because he was having a really bad trip.

As soon as I got back to New York, I had to return to the studio to work on a couple of songs for my second album, *Samantha Fox*. The production was being handled by Full Force, a group of six black guys from Brooklyn who, aside from producing other people's records, also made their own.

One day, when we were working flat out, Paul Stanley came into the studio. I knew that Full Force were working on a remix of one of his songs, but I still froze and didn't know where to look. I was a huge KISS fan, and seeing him there at the mixing deck next to Bow-Legged Lou, I immediately found him attractive.

Yes, he was a lot older than I was, but I'd always been drawn to older people and found them much more interesting than my peers.

I noticed that Paul kept looking in my direction, too, and after he left, Bow-Legged Lou came over and handed me a note with a phone number scrawled on it.

"Paul asked me to give you this and to say you can call him if you want."

I stared at the little scrap of paper and asked, my heart pounding in my chest, "Did he say anything else?"

Bow-Legged Lou shrugged and said, "He asked who you were and then when I told him, he just nodded and said he wanted to meet you."

"Really?"

I walked around with that note in my pocket for several days. In the end, I couldn't resist the temptation, so during a break at the studio one afternoon, I dialed his number.

"Cool that you called," Paul said once I had introduced myself. "I'd almost started to think you never would."

He spoke very well and sounded, on the whole, incredibly polite and friendly, and when he asked whether he could take me out to dinner one evening, I just couldn't say no.

We went on a couple of dates, and before I headed back to England we promised to stay in touch.

On the day I was traveling home, I was waiting for my taxi to JFK in the hotel lobby when a photographer I had worked with in the past came over to me. It was Terry O'Neill (Faye Dunaway's ex-husband). We had a hug and he told me he was with this other guy doing some work for Lionel Richie.

"Hi," the other guy said with a smile. "I just wanted to wish you all the best in your career. I think you've done a great job so far."

I could tell by his accent that he was English, so I said, "Thanks, mate. Are you here on holiday?"

"No, I'm here with work—just like you."

"Aha, what do you do?"

He smiled again. "I play a bit of guitar every now and then."

"Oh, really? What's your name?"

"Eric."

"Eric what?"

"Eric Clapton."

I was so embarrassed, but then he asked if I wanted to come to Lionel Richie's show that night, as he was making a guest appearance. I had to reply that sadly I was leaving for the UK that afternoon.

Back in London, we continued to work on my record and the song that would be my big breakthrough in the US—"Naughty Girls (Need Love Too)."

I put a lot into that project, in more ways than one. Full Force, whom I'd flown over at my own expense, had brought their wives and girlfriends with them—wives and girlfriends whose accommodation I was also expected to cover. The boys also never made it in to the studio before late in the afternoon, by which time I had already been waiting for them for four, maybe five hours.

As if that weren't enough, I'd also rented a sampler from a company I only later realized belonged to my own record label, Jive Records. All we used it for was to sample a guitar solo from a ZZ Top song—after that, it stood in the studio gathering dust for five days, until someone told me it cost a thousand pounds a day to hire. I learned a bitter lesson then, seeing how the costs racked up. I had to pay for the studio time, too.

Still, getting to work with the Full Force guys was great, even if, initially, I didn't really understand what they wanted from the songs they wrote. To begin with, all I got to hear was the beat. It was like there was no real melody, and I said, "We need a hook, a guitar loop. A bit like Santana."

"Santana?" asked Curt-T-T, the group's guitarist, casting a quick glance at the others. Clearly none of them had heard of Santana. "No, no, you don't get it, this is the new thing."

In the end, I finally got a guitar refrain melody and was happy with the result. But then they decided that I should rap on the track.

"Are you crazy? I can't do rapping. How would that sound?"

The fact was, at that point in time, there were no white rappers, particularly not from England. But the guys stood firm—they even wanted me to rap in my own cockney dialect.

"Forget it," I said, holding my hands up in the air. "I'm *not* rapping in cockney, that's that. I'd just sound like those two comedians, Chas and Dave; people would laugh their heads off."

"Come on, Sam," said Bow-Legged Lou. "You could at least try. Why not mix some cockney with a bit of American English, so it sounds all mid-Atlantic?"

"What the hell's mid-Atlantic?" I asked, sounding annoyed, but he simply smiled.

They made me try, in any case, and suddenly I did actually find some kind of hybrid that earned me a thumbs-up from the guys.

"People back home are gonna love this," Bow-Legged Lou reassured me.

I gave him a skeptical look, but he was right. The Americans took that song and turned it into a mega hit, even on the "Black Singles" chart. And no matter where I went in the US, everyone wanted to hear me talk in my dialect. I did hundreds of jingles for US radio stations, just saying the phrase from the beginning of the song: "Maybe, just maybe, naughty girls need love too."

Once the recording of *Naughty Girls* was done, I decided to get to work on something that had been bothering me for a long time: namely that I didn't have a driving license. Taking the last few driving lessons in London, with the paparazzi following my every move, was impossible.

So, I took Mum to the sleepy little beach resort of Llandudno in north Wales and completed a five-day intensive course that actually gave results—because when the time came to take the test, I passed it easily. It meant that when I got back to London, I could finally get behind the wheel of the sports car Peter had given me a few months earlier.

In mid-May, I released a single, "Nothing's Gonna Stop Me Now"—a record that had the super trio of Stock, Aitken, and Waterman behind it. It really did have all of the hallmarks of a song from their successful pop factory.

With that track and the hits from my first record in my arsenal, Dad and I headed to a big music festival in Montreaux a few weeks later. It was some kind of lavish industry event with plenty of stars on offer: the Cure, Simply Red, the Pretenders, Boy George, Alison Moyet, Smokey Robinson, Terence Trent D'Arby, Crowded House, Whitney Houston, and so on.

It was an incredible lineup, and I have to say that I felt pretty insecure when Dad and I attended the pre-press party the night before the festival kicked off. I still felt like I hadn't quite been accepted by the music industry, an impression that was bolstered as

I stepped into the huge, incredibly beautiful hall full of equally beautiful people.

God, everyone in here's so cool, I thought, desperately grabbing a drink from a silver tray being carried by a straight-backed, smiling waiter.

I noticed that people were looking at me, but no one came over to talk to me or to say a few polite words about liking my music.

Dad could see how uncomfortable I was and suggested we sit down on an elegant couch between two French doors at one side.

We sat down and each lit a cigarette (this was back when you could still smoke indoors). I couldn't bring myself to talk to Dad and just stared at all the experienced people—several of whom I had admired for as long as I could remember.

"Is everything OK?" I heard Dad ask.

"Mmm," I lied as I thought to myself: *In their eyes I'm just a page three girl they can't take seriously.*

Right then, I saw Chrissie Hynde of the Pretenders coming straight towards me with an ashtray. She held it out and came to a halt in front of me.

"Thought you might need this," she said with a smile.

"Thanks," I said, sounding surprised. I tapped the ash from my cigarette.

I had long been a fan of the Pretenders, and now Chrissie Hynde, one of the coolest women on earth, was talking to *me*. I could hardly believe it was true.

"I've been following you," she said, sitting down next to me. "You've really got something." She smiled again and looked out at the other people in the room before she continued, "There might be people in here who think you're just a flash in the pan that they don't need to worry about, but you should forget all that. I heard you in rehearsal today, and man, you've got a voice!"

I could feel myself blushing with happiness. With just a few words and the warmth of her character, she'd given me my self-confidence back.

The next day, I had to do a load of newspaper, radio, and TV interviews before I could head to the concert hall for another rehearsal.

Dad had kicked out the press. The show was going to be broadcast on TV, and I didn't want to be distracted by a crowd of journalists while I listened to directions from the cameramen and producer.

But just as I'd sung "Nothing's Gonna Stop Me Now" for maybe the third time, I noticed, out of the corner of my eye, two girls watching me from the side of the stage. One was black and the other was white. I was annoyed, because I assumed they were journalists and didn't want them there while I rehearsed. But when I looked over to Dad and nodded in the girls' direction, he simply mimed, "Don't worry, it's OK."

Then, when I left the stage, he came over to me and said, "Sammy, I want you to meet Whitney Houston and her assistant Robyn Crawford."

I hadn't recognized my idol, Whitney, and I had no idea what to say when she came over and shook my hand.

It turned out that Whitney had watched my entire rehearsal, even though it had been going on for an hour or so, and now she asked for my autograph. The whole thing felt completely surreal, of course, but I still managed to compose myself enough to ask, "Could I get your autograph?"

"Sure, honey," she smiled, and then she wrote:

To baby Sam, you're so cute.
God bless you.
Love,
Whitney

I tried not to show how touched I was when she handed me the note.

Whitney was one of the few artists who got to sing live that evening. I myself did singback—or, in other words, I sang over the original.

Someone who mimed completely and took the opportunity to launch her single "Boys, Boys, Boys," was Sabrina. She had already said a load of crap about me in the papers, and when I told that to Taylor Dane, whom I kind of hooked up with there since we were both newcomers in the industry, she flared up. Taylor was a tough New York girl, and she wanted to beat Sabrina up there and then.

I could just see the headlines, so I said, "That's probably not a good idea."

Taylor said, "She's just jealous, Sam."

Subsequently, I became good friends with Sabrina, but more on that later.

After my performance, as I sat down in my dressing room to take a breather, I was about to have another surreal meeting. There was a knock at the door, and Dad opened it a little. From where I was sitting at my dressing table, I saw the color drain from his face. It was like he had seen a ghost. He looked over to me and tried to mime something as he talked with the person outside. I didn't understand a thing. Above all, I didn't know why he looked so strange.

"What? Who is it?" I whispered.

Right then, he started to whistle a tune as quietly as he could— also trying to keep the conversation going with whoever it was he was talking to. The whole thing just got stranger and stranger, but suddenly I recognised the old soul hit "Tears of a Clown"!

"Smokey Robinson?" I whispered.

Dad mimed "Yes!" and jerked his head for me to come over to the doorway.

I quickly got up and went over to say hello.

"Hi, I'm Smokey, nice to meet you," he said, smiling broadly and holding out a hand.

Things became strange again after that, because he asked for a photo with me. Yes, I was fairly big in America by that point, but it still felt completely insane that someone like Smokey was asking for a picture. And things would get even weirder. After I signed my name and wrote a little greeting to him on a picture that Dad had quickly handed me, Smokey leaned in and said, with a smile, "Could I please ask you to wear my jacket for just a little while? I want it to smell like you when I take it back to America."

I just stared at him as he started to take off his pale-blue jacket. Was he messing with me? I gave Dad a helpless glance, but he was no help, he just stood there staring adoringly at Smokey, who now held out his jacket to me.

"You put my jacket on, 'cause then I can prove it's really you." His face cracked into another wide smile. "You got a smell, Foxy!"

Still feeling like the whole thing must be a bad joke, I took his jacket and pulled it on.

Smokey looked incredibly happy—Dad, too.

Once Smokey had taken back his jacket and left with his 6 foot 5, three-hundred-pound bodyguard, I turned to Dad and said, "What was that?!"

I could hear that I sounded a little shocked—and also a little annoyed.

"That . . ." Dad said, his eyes following Smokey rather than looking at me, ". . . is a living legend."

13

SCANDINAVIA

People were so drunk that they were falling headlong
out of the trees they had climbed to get a better view.
Others fell where they were standing and then lay
still on the ground as other people stepped over them,
completely unconcerned. Kids who looked no older than
twelve or thirteen were staggering around with huge
bottles of vodka, shouting loudly.

The very thing I'd been so afraid of throughout my childhood finally happened in early summer 1987. My parents decided that they no longer wanted to live together. Or, more accurately, Mum decided she no longer wanted to live with Dad, and in some way it was all my fault. In any case, I blamed myself for our family falling apart.

Yes, their relationship had been turbulent from day one, and there had been long periods where they were married only on paper. During those times, it was like they were in completely different places, even though they physically lived beneath the same roof. But it still came as a shock when Mum turned to me and said, "I've told your dad I don't want to live with him anymore."

We were in the kitchen in the house in Hertfordshire, where I had barely spent a single night since I'd bought it, I'd been in the US with work so often. Those few days I was back in London, I always thought it took too long to drive out there and would stay at the small flat I owned in town, instead. Or else I'd stay with Peter, who rented a small mansion not far from my place in the countryside.

But Mum and Vanessa lived in the house, as Dad occasionally did, too. Though now he was no longer welcome and had to go back to our old house.

"You've been married so long," I said, feeling my stomach lurch.

Mum sighed. "Sammy, you know what your dad's like, and now his drinking's gone so far I don't want to be with him anymore."

It was true that Dad's drinking was getting out of control. I'd also noticed that he had started doing a lot of coke during our work trips.

Mum looked up at me. "He tried to smother me with a cushion during our latest fight."

I swallowed and didn't really know what to say. Suddenly, I realized that by buying this house, I had given Mum the opportunity to leave Dad—something she had probably been waiting to do for a very long time. As long as they lived together in the house in Crouch End, she was completely dependent on him. I mean, she didn't even have her own bank account.

"If I weren't famous, this never would have happened," I mumbled. "We would still be a family."

Mum took my hand and shook her head. "No, Sammy, we wouldn't. Things have been over between us for a long time."

I knew I had to accept that fact, but it still felt incredibly difficult to get up in front of the TV cameras and millions of viewers a few days later, and give a professional rendition of "Nothing's Gonna Stop Me Now" on *Top of the Pops*.

Someone who really couldn't accept that fact was Dad, who suddenly started turning up at the house with flowers, standing on the steps to the porch and pleading and begging Mum to give him and their marriage another chance.

But Mum just said, "It's too late, Pat," and then closed the door in his face.

Just as all this was happening, I had to go on a summer tour to Finland, where I'd topped both the singles and album charts and had a mega hit with "Nothing's Gonna Stop Me Now." The single was sold out everywhere and we toured the entire country, eventually coming so far north that we were within the Arctic Circle, where I was headlining the Midnight Sun Festival.

The sun really did never go down at that time of year, which was pretty crazy. But seeing the audience was even crazier.

The organizers had hired a Rolls Royce for me to arrive in, and they'd draped a huge British flag across it. In bright sunshine, late at night, I was driven to the huge field where an outdoor stage had been built. As the car pulled up, so many people came staggering over to us that I thought we would run someone over. When I got out, I could hardly make it up onto the stage because the fans were literally fighting one another to get the chance to see me and touch me.

"Jesus Christ, what is this place?" I asked my guitarist in terror once I'd made it up the steps unscathed.

"The north of Finland," he said in a tone that suggested it wasn't his first time there.

We got started with the gig, and complete chaos immediately broke out in the crowd. People were forcing their way towards the stage, meaning that those at the front were being crushed against the barriers. Several people were actually so badly injured that we had to stop the show after a couple of songs so that they could be carried out and taken away in ambulances.

"Can we really go on?" I asked my keyboardist as one of the organizers waved for us to start up again.

But rather than replying, he just nodded towards the crowd. I followed his gaze and what I saw was one of the craziest things I had ever seen—and probably will ever see—during my entire career.

People were so drunk that they were falling headlong out of the trees they had climbed to get a better view. Others fell where they were standing and then lay still on the ground as other people stepped over them, completely unconcerned. Kids who looked no older than twelve or thirteen were staggering around with huge bottles of vodka, shouting loudly. But the worst part was that I could see people having sex in the crowd, without a single care that anyone might see what they were doing.

When I arrived in Hunnebostrand on the west coast of Sweden a week or so later, the audience also acted oddly. Suddenly, midway through the gig, they started throwing coins at me.

Who are these idiots? I thought, ducking as best I could.

What I didn't know was that the promoter had advertised the gig as a proper concert, while Dad and I had agreed with him that I would just perform three songs with playback. So maybe it wasn't so strange that the audience was angry, even if the whole idea of throwing coins still confuses me. In any case, I was furious at the promoter for promising the crowd something he hadn't paid me for.

"You're making them hate me when really it's you they should be throwing things at," I shouted the minute I spotted him after more or less fleeing the stage.

Arriving at the recording of a Swedish TV program for children and teenagers, *Solstollarna*, felt much more comfortable.

I was flown in a helicopter onto a beach where it was being shot, and I remember turning to my bodyguard Dave, who was sitting behind me. "Great, isn't it?"

Dave nodded with a satisfied expression, and when we landed he ran a hand through his bleached blond hair before stepping out of the helicopter in his white trousers and tight, pale-blue sweater. Dave really was particular about his appearance, and he did everything he could to look like his great idol, Don Johnson.

In any case, we got started with the recording on the beach right away, and I was standing next to one of the presenters when I suddenly spotted Dave lying back in a jacuzzi, surrounded by a group of young Swedish girls in bikinis.

"What're you up to?" I shouted to my so-called bodyguard, who, at that moment at least, wasn't doing much for his wages.

"They wanted me to lie here and relax in the background while you were doing whatever you're doing," he shouted back. Then his entire face lit up in a smile and he shouted, "I love this job!"

In Sweden—though I wasn't aware of it to begin with—my image as an artist was different to the majority of other countries, and that was all down to the Swedish idol magazine *Okej*. I'd appeared in practically every edition of it—often on the cover. In fact, it was *Okej* that had helped to establish me in Sweden. The only problem was that the pictures they published were the topless ones from the beginning of my career as a glamour model, and though I wasn't ashamed of those images, it felt strange to be using them then, especially considering the magazine's readers were primarily children.

"Guess they're just a bit more liberal than us," my bassist said when I showed him the magazine.

Maybe he was right, because they did the same thing in West Germany. In Britain, having those pictures in that kind of magazine was unthinkable.

That entire summer was incredibly busy, because "Nothing's Gonna Stop Me Now" climbed the charts in a number of countries, soon becoming the second highest-selling single across Europe. But apparently I was also popular behind the Iron Curtain, in the Eastern Bloc countries, because one day, Dad called and said, "You're never going to believe this, Sammy."

"What?"

"You've started getting bags of mail from fans in the USSR."

"But I haven't released anything there," I said, surprised.

"No, the records get smuggled in and end up on the black market. I've got friends who say they've made a fortune from the signed records I gave them. One of them came over and showed me the bottles of vodka and tins of black caviar he got from a couple of Russian sailors in exchange for a signed poster and a T-shirt with your signature on it. He said the Russians are completely crazy about you."

"Oh!" I said, but honestly, I didn't understand how they could be such huge fans when they had never seen me live or on TV. In the West, on the other hand, "Nothing's Gonna Stop Me Now" was being shown almost constantly on TV, and by the end of the year it would be the fourth most played video. I'd shot it in Marbella in Spain in early May. The sea was anything but warm at the time, but the director still wanted me in the water, pretending to enjoy it. In truth, I was freezing!

That made it all the better to get away to Australia on a well-deserved beach holiday in early September. I went with Peter, Mum, and two blokes from my neighborhood, Vince and Terry.

I'd known Vince since I was a kid, when we were living in Morgan Mansions. Just a few weeks after I bought the house in Hertfordshire, I bumped into him on the street.

"You're a handy geezer, aren't you?" I said to him. "You couldn't come and fix up a few things in my new house? You know, stuff I can't do myself or don't have time to take care of?"

"Sure," he said without hesitation.

And when he came round to start tinkering about in the house, putting up shelves, installing a dishwasher, and that kind of thing, he met Peter. The two of them quickly realized they were on the same wavelength, and when Peter later met our old friend Terry, he was just as keen on him.

Peter liked to be surrounded by a little entourage, and Vince and Terry started coming with us whenever we went out. As always, Peter paid for everyone, and to me it was obvious what he was doing.

"Peter," I said one night when we were out at a nightclub, "you can't keep doing that. You're buying people. They're not real friends."

But he just shrugged, and it made me furious. Mostly, it annoyed me that he always had to have a little gang with him, like just being with me wasn't enough. But since we were at our local and had other people's eyes on us, I didn't cause a scene. At least not that time.

It was as though Peter wanted to feel like the Godfather himself. Powerful and respected—maybe even feared, what do I know? In my eyes, it was childish and insecure behaviour, and when he told me that he'd asked Vince and Terry to come with us to Australia, I was so disappointed I couldn't hide it.

Peter could see how dark my eyes became, and he hurried to say, "But babe, your mum's coming, too. And I do actually need a bodyguard to take care of the money." He was talking about the briefcase full of cash for unforeseen expenses that he always took with him on trips. "Vince is perfect for that." He stepped forward and took hold of my upper arms with what I'm sure he hoped was a charming smile. "And Terry's always a laugh!"

So, as we—Peter, Mum, Vince, Terry, and I—traveled to Brisbane and then on to the coastal town and holiday paradise of Gold Coast, I had an increasingly strong feeling that Peter cared more about himself than about our relationship. I even had a nagging suspicion that his business came before me, not that he would have admitted it, even with a gun to his head.

Why, I asked myself as I sat there in my plane seat, pretending to read a monthly magazine, *why else would I have this feeling that he's exploiting me?* I mean, could I really trust Peter? Was he really thinking of what was best for me when he launched all those products using my face and my name? Was it out of love that he was bringing me into all those business deals?

I glanced at Peter, who was laughing at something Terry had just said.

Was this the man who would support me through difficult periods like the one I was experiencing right then, with my parents' divorce? Was he strong enough to give me the security I needed now that my family had been split in two? Just before we left, Vanessa had decided that she missed her friends and moved in with Dad in Crouch End, so our family really was split right down the middle now.

I looked over to Mum, who was sitting across the aisle with her eyes closed, seemingly asleep. It was she, not Peter, who was my biggest support whenever I felt weak. Just as I tried to support her after her separation from Dad.

I sighed. I had thought that the trip could be a good opportunity for Mum and me to talk through what had happened to our family in peace and quiet. Instead, it felt like we were tagging along on an excursion with the lads. Those weeks in the sun, which until recently had seemed so tempting, suddenly lost all appeal and meaning.

What am I doing here? I thought, which is obviously an awful thought to think as you're sitting next to your boyfriend on the way to a long, romantic holiday on the other side of the world.

But once we arrived, things didn't feel especially romantic. Despite the perfect external circumstances, I'd have to describe the mood as increasingly irritated. Peter had rented a yacht with all the comforts you could wish for, and we sailed out to the Great Barrier Reef, where we had thought we would be left in peace to enjoy the sun, sea, and sky. But we were fooling ourselves, because a number of boats suddenly appeared from nowhere, full of journalists and paparazzi, swarming around us like huge flies we couldn't shake off.

That didn't exactly improve the mood on board, despite Terry's attempts to cheer us up with his jokes and pranks. But it was like something unstoppable had been set in motion, and I suddenly heard myself snapping at Peter for so often allowing his jealousy to poison our relationship.

"No man owns me, do you hear that?"

Both Vince and Terry suddenly looked like they wished they were somewhere very different from that luxury boat floating on still, turquoise waters with a clear blue sky above. Mum looked more concerned, but she also said—in private—that she understood how I felt.

One evening, with the most perfect romantic moonlight on the water, I realized that enough was enough.

"I don't think I can go through with it anymore," I said to Peter as we sat alone on the afterdeck looking out at the calm sea.

Peter turned to me, and for once, in the faint light of the yacht, he looked completely resigned. "I know exactly what you mean."

We didn't need to say any more after that. We were done with one another, and our last few days at sea were pretty calm. Suddenly, there was no reason to annoy one another or to start bickering.

The night before Mum and I were due to fly back to England, Peter and I went out to eat at a restaurant in Gold Coast. It was some kind of goodbye dinner, and as we sat there making small talk, I struggled to work out whether I felt more sad or relieved that it was over.

But the next day, after he gave Mum and me a ride to the airport in Brisbane and we were about to part ways, it was the sorrow that felt worse after all. Peter kissed me and said, "Bye, Sammy."

I said, "Bye, Peter," then quickly turned and walked towards the gate.

14

PAUL STANLEY

Once I became famous, the men I was with always
thought they were going to bed with Samantha Fox,
and I always felt like I had to step into that role . . .
to perform in bed. I just didn't want whoever I was
with to think I was a bad shag and pass that on.

After my breakup with Peter, I really was down. To begin with, I thought it was about him, but as time passed I realized it was more that I missed being being close to someone. Maybe that was why, after things with Peter ended, I called Paul.

He sounded happy to hear from me and said, "Why don't you come over to New York this weekend? I'm only in the studio for a couple of hours during the day—we'd have plenty of time to hang out."

I liked Paul, and though we had only been on a few dates, I felt like I missed him.

"I'd love to," I said. "I have a few things to sort out today, but I could fly tomorrow."

I landed at John F. Kennedy International Airport the very next day, and Paul was waiting outside the terminal with his brand-new Porsche. He really did seem glad to see me and gave me a quick kiss on the lips before he opened the passenger side door.

"Check this out," he said, pointing.

I followed the line of his finger, and for a moment I thought he had spread an animal skin over the floor of the car.

"Lambskin," he said, gesturing for me to climb in.

We tore off, Paul put on some good music, and everything felt great. Or it did until he suddenly wrinkled his nose and said, "What's that smell?'

Right then, I also noticed that something stank.

"Could it be from the cars outside?" I wondered.

"Nah, it's something else," Paul said, glancing over as though he thought it was me who smelled bad.

I glanced nervously into my handbag, which was by my feet, worried I'd forgotten about something edible inside. But instead, to my horror, I realized that I must have stepped in dog shit outside the airport, and that I'd managed to smear it into the cream-coloured lambskin that matched the color scheme of the rest of the car. I froze and thought, *Help me now . . . I haven't even made it to his place yet and this happens.*

"Erm . . . I think I . . . um . . . stepped in some dog shit," I said, wanting the seat to swallow me up.

Paul gave me a wide-eyed look and then glanced at my feet. He quickly composed himself again and gave me a forced smile as he said, "These things happen."

Paul had a huge apartment not far from Central Park, and the view really was incredible, particularly from the living room, which had panoramic windows in every direction. It felt like you could see the whole of New York from up there.

But as he showed me around his place, I quickly realized we were very different. He was much tidier than me and even hung the clothes in his enormous walk-in closet in color order. I thought it seemed more like an incredibly luxurious hotel suite than a home, and the perfect neatness immediately made me unsure and a little tense. Things didn't get any better when the dull ache I'd felt in a molar during the long flight started to really hurt.

"Are you OK?" Paul asked, knitting his dark, well-groomed brows as we sat at the dining table in the living room with candles and a beautifully presented supper in front of us, while dusk fell over the city on the other side of the panoramic windows.

"It's nothing, just a bit of toothache," I said, taking a sip of incredibly expensive wine. I didn't want him to worry or to ruin the romantic mood we were both so keen on.

But though I did everything I could to ignore it, the pain just wouldn't go away. Instead, it turned into some kind of monster that wanted to kill me and get in the way with Paul.

"I'm sorry, but I don't think I can," I said unhappily as we lay between the crisp silk sheets in his bed. "My tooth hurts so much." I knew it sounded like a bad excuse, especially since we still hadn't slept together and I was worried he would think I was reserved, inexperienced, or just unsure.

Once I became famous, the men I was with always thought they were going to bed with Samantha Fox, and I always felt like I had to step into that role . . . to perform in bed. I just didn't want whoever I was with to think I was a bad shag and pass that on. Many of the men I slept with also had really strange ideas about me, and thought that the longer they could hold out, the better they were as a lover. So I quickly learned a lot about giving oral sex, since that was the quickest and simplest way of sorting things out. The problem was that I got so good at it that they fell even more in love with something I didn't enjoy that much.

"I'll drive you to my dentist tomorrow," Paul said, interrupting my thoughts. "I'll call her as soon as I wake up."

He gave me a tender kiss and thankfully didn't seem either annoyed or disappointed. I took a couple of painkillers and then lay there in bed with my mind spinning. I was suddenly worried that Paul, who was quite a bit older than me, would think I was some hopeless kid he didn't have time for. But then the pills finally started to work, and I fell asleep from pure exhaustion.

When I woke the next morning, Paul had already managed to prepare breakfast, and as he poured me a cup of tea he said that his dentist had promised to see me right away.

"Thanks; it's nice of you to organize it so quickly," I said, my hand cupping my cheek. Paul gave me a sympathetic look, and once I had drunk my tea he drove me straight to the dentist, a middle-aged woman with a warm smile. Paul kissed me on the cheek and told me he would see me back at his apartment once he was done in the studio, and I followed the woman into her office.

I didn't have time to do much more than open my mouth before she decided that I had a wisdom tooth that needed extracting. She quickly got to work. It took quite a bit of force and even more local anesthetic, so when I finally left I felt both like I'd been punched and like my face was paralyzed. I was very grateful that Paul hadn't made it back to his apartment by the time I got there.

"He can't see me like this," I slurred to my reflection in the bathroom mirror.

I really did look like an idiot, with my mouth drooping at an angle and saliva running from one corner, no matter how hard I tried to suck it back in. When the anesthetic started to wear off, the tooth still hurt, despite all the painkillers I was taking. To keep myself from going crazy with pain, I decided to clean the flat. I hunted down the vacuum cleaner and set to work on the floor in the living room. Hanging by each of the panoramic windows, Paul had pale, floor-length muslin curtains. Now, I'm clumsy even at the best of times, but my motor skills and ability to concentrate weren't exactly helped by the pain I was in and the medications I'd taken.

Before I had time to react, one of the long, flimsy curtains was suddenly sucked into the vacuum cleaner's nozzle. The next thing I knew, the entire curtain had been torn from the metal rod above the window. It rattled as the curtain quickly came loose from ring after ring and then fell onto me, meaning I could barely see what I was doing.

While I used my free hand to try to push the curtain from my face, I desperately stamped on the vacuum cleaner to try to turn it off, but in doing so I accidentally pointed the nozzle at another curtain, which also got sucked up and started to come loose from the rail.

Just as I managed to free myself from the first curtain, the second one elegantly fell to the floor as the vacuum cleaner suddenly went quiet.

"Jesus, what have I done?" I mumbled, staring at the crumpled curtains by my feet.

I ran to the kitchen to fetch a bar stool, but even when I climbed up onto it, I wasn't tall enough to reach the curtain rail and rehang the curtains.

I had no choice but to leave them in a pile on the floor, and when Paul got home a while later he jumpily exclaimed, "What happened to my curtains?!"

I squirmed in my seat on the sofa.

"I just wanted to tidy up," I said, still slurring slightly.

Paul looked at me as though he didn't quite know what to think.

But he seemed to forgive me for my clumsiness all the same, because we slept together for the first time that night. And though Paul might not exactly have been marriage material, he had slept with so many women that he really did know what he was doing. Looking back now, I can say that he was, without a doubt, one of the best male lovers I've ever had or will have. And that's despite the fact that he had certain habits that confused me . . . like tearing off the condom the minute we were done and jumping into the shower, leaving me lying there in bed, feeling dirty.

The pain was gone when I woke the next morning, and I was happy about both that and the fact that Paul and I had consummated our relationship, so to speak. Lying on my stomach with my eyes still closed, I reached out to touch him. My fingers found his hair and stroked it, but then it felt as though the hair had come loose. Terrified, I pulled back my hand and realized I was holding Paul's hair extensions. Equally horrified, I turned to his side and realized I was alone in the big double bed.

Once again, I looked down at the long, black wisps of hair that Paul must have stuffed beneath his pillow. At that very moment, I heard a sound from the bathroom and realized that he had just stepped out of the shower and would be back in the bedroom any second. I froze in panic and didn't know what to do with the hair. All I knew was that Paul would think I was a real weirdo if he came in and saw me sitting there holding it.

I glanced around the room, which was so spotless and minimally decorated that there weren't really any good hiding places. I could hear footsteps approaching, and without thinking I leaned over the edge of the bed and threw the hair beneath it. I had just managed to haul myself back into a half-lying position when Paul came into the room.

"Morning!" he said, stepping into a golden g-string. I'd never seen a man wear a thong before, so I didn't really know where to look.

"I have to go to the studio, but I'll make breakfast for us first," Paul smiled.

I reciprocated the smile and then the kiss he gave me.

While Paul was at the studio, I decided to go shopping, and I quickly found a shop full of imported English goods. I made up my mind that the next morning, I would treat Paul to breakfast as thanks for making it for me two days in a row. It would also be a good way to ease my bad conscience at having ripped down his curtains.

The only problem was that I made another mistake that very same evening, when I took a glass of water into the bedroom and set it down on the bedside table at my side of the bed.

"What are you doing?!" Paul shouted when he saw. "You can't put that glass there. The table's an antique, five hundred years old; it cost fifteen thousand dollars. It'll leave an ugly ring on the wood if you put the glass there."

"Ah . . . sorry," I said, quickly grabbing the glass and accidentally causing some of the water to slosh onto the table. Paul's eyes widened in some kind of horror and I got so nervous that I grabbed my pillow to wipe up the little pool. But as I did that, I almost knocked over the bedside lamp, which was probably also very old and very expensive.

Paul sighed and rolled his eyes, making me feel like a bull in a china shop, though I was anything but big.

The next morning, I snuck out into the kitchen before he woke, and sleepily started to prepare an English breakfast.

The only thing was, as I tried to pour sugar into a bowl, I managed to spill most of it on the floor. And just as I was busy cleaning it up with a cloth, I heard a noise from the microwave, where I was heating a bowl of baked beans. I'd completely forgotten about them—I still wasn't really awake yet.

Before I made it over to the microwave, it suddenly shook with a violent explosion, and the inside of the glass door was covered in a reddish-yellow mess. Somehow, the beans had exploded.

"What are you doing?" I heard Paul ask behind me.

I spun around and met his eye. He was already dressed to leave for the studio, and now his eyes darted from my face to the microwave.

"English breakfast," I said with a strained smile.

"Jesus Christ," he said, taking a few steps forward to inspect the damage more closely.

The floor crunched beneath his boots, and he stopped mid-step, wondering why there was sugar all over the floor. I flashed him an equal parts innocent and uncomprehending look.

"I don't know."

"Hmm," Paul said, opening the microwave oven.

"I'll take care of it," I blurted out.

Paul sighed and went out into the living room. I rushed to make a cup of instant coffee, added a splash of milk, and quickly buttered some bread. Then I took everything out to Paul.

"Here you go," I said, flashing him my most loving smile.

Paul looked down at the cup.

"Is that soy milk?"

"Erm . . . I don't know. I can go and check," I said, hurrying back to the kitchen.

"Also," he shouted after me, "check you used the gluten-free bread."

Once Paul had everything he wanted, I finished cleaning the microwave. I was pretty pleased with the finished result, but the same didn't seem to be true of Paul.

"I hope you've cleaned it properly," he said when he came into the room, peering suspiciously over my shoulder.

"I *have* cleaned it," I reassured him.

He still didn't seem convinced, and said, "If you don't clean it properly, it won't cook food as well."

All I could do was start again, while Paul disappeared to the studio. I was meant to be flying back to London two days later, but when Paul got home that afternoon, I said, "I'm sorry, but I have to go home as soon as possible. Dad's got appendicitis; he's in hospital. Mum says it's really bad and that he needs an operation, so I want to be there for him."

It was a lie, of course, something I'm not proud of. But right there and then, I didn't feel like I could stay at Paul's any longer. Considering everything that had already happened, I was worried about causing more, and worse, accidents if I stayed.

"I'm sorry to hear that," said Paul. "I can check when the next flight to London leaves and give you a ride to the airport."

"Thanks," I said, feeling even guiltier at how considerate he was being.

Paul and I continued to see one another, even though long periods of time might pass between dates. There weren't many gaps in our work schedules, and we often found ourselves in completely different countries. When we finally got together, for example, KISS were on a huge world tour, so I took the opportunity to see him either when they had a break between dates or when they were performing somewhere I could get to. Like the time they were headlining the Monsters of Rock festival at Donington Park in the UK.

I headed up there with Dad, his friend Neil, and my friend Julie, whom I'd known since I saved her from a gossip writer at a wine bar on Fleet Street. I had watched the journalist plying her with champagne and then saw her stagger to the toilet. When I went out there myself a while later, I heard her throwing up in one of the cubicles.

"Are you OK?" I asked, getting a groan in reply.

She let me in, in any case, and I looked after her, asked what her name was. I said, "I don't know what story you're doing, but you should really go home."

After that, I smuggled her out the back entrance, hailed a black cab, gave the driver ten pounds, and managed to get the address out of Julie. A few months later, I bumped into her at the opening of a nightclub called the Limelight. She hugged me and thanked me for what I had done, and we'd been friends ever since.

At Donington Park, she came with me to see Paul just before KISS were about to perform. He was wearing his stage makeup and costume, and after Julie and I had made our way back to the VIP area in front of the stage, she gave me a concerned look and said, "You know, I'm not sure he's right for you."

But the moment KISS got started and Paul transformed into his stage persona, Starchild, in front of maybe a hundred thousand screaming fans, she changed her mind and turned to me with a smile: "Now I see what you mean!"

But there was one person who wasn't impressed by Paul's performance, and that was Dad, who leaned in to me mid-concert and said, "He looks like Tiny bloody Tim."

Anyone who has seen the ukulele player will know that it wasn't a particularly kind remark, but Dad had never liked any of my boyfriends.

I didn't care what he thought and was determined to enjoy my first rock festival, and once KISS finished their set I went backstage to be with Paul.

I was a little nervous, because it was the first time I had met the rest of the band.

"Your new girl?" Gene Simmons asked, taking my hand as he gave Paul a slightly ambiguous smile.

I immediately got the feeling that Gene saw me as nothing but one in a line of Paul's many girls, a young tart, even. And that impression only got stronger when I saw him again, later, in New York. Paul and I went out to eat with him a few times, and he talked to me as though I wasn't an adult, more as though he thought I was someone he didn't need to take seriously or care about. It didn't feel good, and even if I did get on OK with Gene, he also scared me. He had an incredibly dry sense of humor that I never really knew how to take.

Just like Paul, Gene was pretty quiet and calm as a person—the opposite of what you would expect once you'd seen him on stage. There wasn't much that was rock 'n' roll about any of them when you spent time with them in private. Both were well-educated men from middle-class families and might even seem a bit boring to someone like me, who came from a place where things were more lively and jokey. Plus, in my opinion, they dressed like old men. Paul often wore suits in his spare time.

"Suit again?" I would ask, sounding disappointed, when he came to meet me wearing those clothes.

"Yeah?" He sounded completely uncomprehending.

At times like that, I didn't have the energy to explain that I preferred the rock star to the businessman. But sometimes I still made little attempts to get what I wanted.

"Aren't you going to wear eyeliner?" I asked a couple of times, since I thought he looked much better in a bit of makeup and wanted him to wear it in private.

"What, do you think I need it?" he asked, sounding slightly worried.

Paul's best friend was Michael Bolton, the singer, and we often went out to eat with him when I was staying in New York. He'd started out as a hard rock singer and actually even auditioned to be in Black Sabbath, but at the time we hung out he was in the middle of his transition to becoming a superstar with his ballads. In private, he was about as rock 'n' roll as Paul and Gene—in other words, not at all. But, unlike Gene, Michael did at least make me feel at ease.

You couldn't exactly say the same of my first dinner with Paul's parents. Paul thought that our relationship had been going on for a sufficient amount of time, and was serious enough, to have reached the point where a good Jewish boy from Queens had to introduce his girlfriend to Mom and Dad. They had been asking about me, too, apparently, and had shown a strong desire to meet me. So I didn't really have a choice.

The day before we would be having dinner with them, Paul came home with a couple of huge shopping bags from Barneys.

"I bought some clothes I thought you could wear tomorrow," he said, quickly pulling out a very conservative pink cashmere jacket from one bag.

He had bought me presents before, but this was the first time he had ever given me clothing, and something about the way he was doing it told me that there was an ulterior motive to his generosity.

"And this is to match," he said, pulling out an equally pink and equally proper skirt from the other bag. Again, made from cashmere.

I didn't really know what to say, and all I managed was a slightly hesitant "Thanks."

"Try them," Paul said with an encouraging smile.

I did as he wanted, and as I studied myself in the mirror it was like looking at another person. I looked like a secretary from some flashy New York office, but I also had to admit that the pieces were nice. Paul had clearly taken a lot of care in choosing them, and he seemed incredibly pleased.

"They really suit you," he said, reminding me of Professor Higgins in *My Fair Lady*.

He wants to dress me up and make me over, just like Higgins did with Eliza, so that he can show me off to his parents, I thought.

To test him a little, I said, "Can't I just wear my ordinary clothes?"

My ordinary clothes were a leather jacket and jeans with ripped knees.

"That's probably not a good idea," said Paul. "I know my mother will like these, and I want you to make a good impression."

Being the tomboy I was, I felt uncomfortable dressed up as some kind of living doll. But at the same time, wearing those clothes for one evening felt like a small price to pay. Clearly, it was important to Paul, and I could just be happy that, unlike Higgins, he hadn't tried to erase my cockney accent.

So, the next evening, wearing my little pink jacket and little pink skirt, I arrived at the restaurant in Little Italy where Paul's parents were waiting for us. I was incredibly nervous because I was convinced that they would see through my disguise and decide that I wasn't good enough for their son.

But they were actually very friendly and I quickly relaxed, especially once I got a couple of glasses of white wine in me. Paul ordered clams in tomato sauce with garlic for everyone, which worried me slightly because I had never eaten them before. I had just raised a tentative forkful to my mouth when Paul's mother turned to me and said, "So, Samantha, you're an artist, too?"

I nodded with my hand over my mouth, quickly swallowed my mouthful, and replied, "Yes, but nowhere near as successful as Paul."

Apparently it was a good answer—it was both modest and gave his mum, Eva, and dad, William, the opportunity to look proudly at their son.

Paul turned to me with a warm look in his eyes and said, "Come on, Sam, you've actually been higher up the *Billboard* charts than me."

In the end, it was a really pleasant evening, and as we left the restaurant I remember feeling like I had passed the test after all.

15

NAUGHTY GIRLS NEED LOVE, TOO

My heart was pounding in my chest, and it felt like
muscle after muscle in my body was going numb.
The band kept playing and I tried again, but all
that came from my mouth was air.

On February 8, 1988, when I was nominated alongside Kate Bush, Alison Moyet, Sinitta, and Kim Wilde in the category of British Female Solo Artist at the Brit Awards, I had come further in my music career than I ever could have dreamed. Even if I didn't win the prize that evening, it was an enormous recognition, topped off by the fact that my new album was heading up the charts all around the world.

Maybe that was why things hit me so hard that spring.

The first thing that happened was Kit Miller and Peter Foster, my ex-boyfriends, selling the details of my love life to the press—Kit to the *Sun* and Peter to *Playboy*.

The two men had met through me, and had since started working together on Peter's health products.

In Peter's interview, he claimed, among other things, that I had forced him to have sex up to five times a day; Kit said that during our relationship, I'd had sex with another page three girl. None of it was true, but constantly being linked to the two of them started to get incredibly irritating, not least because some people assumed I knew all about their scams, or that I was even participating in them. At that particular moment, they were busy launching a new product called Slim-liner, and the interview Kit gave to the *Sun* must have been part of the launch, because he wasn't paid for it. Instead, he was given free publicity for his and Peter's products in exchange for making up stories about me.

The next blow came during a break from a PR tour in the US, when I flew to Italy to do a couple of gigs there. I'll never forget it. Right in the middle of a show, my voice started to disappear, and I suddenly found myself unable to sing a single note. I saw a couple of people at the front look up at me in confusion and felt an almost surreal sense of unease spread through my body.

I'd noticed the problem before. It was like I constantly had a cold, and I had realized that my voice was getting deeper and deeper.

I looked out at the crowd, who were roaring my name in unison. My heart was pounding in my chest, and it felt like muscle after muscle in my body was going numb. The band kept playing and I tried again, but all that came from my mouth was air. Shortly afterwards, I ran from the stage.

Mum met me in the backstage area, and when she realized what was happening, she immediately booked two seats on the last flight to London. We slept over at her house that night, and she called our GP the very next morning, who recommended a Harley Street throat specialist.

The doctor's office was one of those sterile rooms with white walls and thin cracks in the ceiling. The smell of disinfectant also made me feel nauseous.

The doctor looked like doctors often do, and once he welcomed us in and Mum and I sat down opposite him, he started to examine my throat in silence.

"Mmm," he mumbled after a while. "You have four nodules on one of your vocal cords, and there's two more developing."

Mum and I glanced at one another.

"What?" I managed to whisper with a great deal of effort.

The doctor settled back in his chair and gave me a stern look.

"Your larynx is also infected."

I had heard that Elton John, Rod Stewart, and Bonnie Tyler had all had similar problems after touring nonstop, but I had never in my wildest imagination thought it might happen to me. I mean, I was twenty-one and had only been singing for two years.

"I'm afraid that operating is the only option," the doctor continued.

I looked at Mum, who couldn't hide her anxiety when she asked, "What are the chances of her voice returning to normal?"

"Impossible to say," the doctor replied, turning to me. "You need to prepare yourself for the possibility that you might never be able to sing again."

I had the operation in early March, and when I woke up afterwards, I was told that I had to be completely silent for three weeks. It was only then that the doctor would be able to see whether the operation had been a success.

I was meant to be going back to the US to do yet more PR work for my new single, "Naughty Girls Need Love Too." There were also plans for me to record a video for the track. But I had no choice but to put everything back a month.

Those few weeks were incredibly anxious and difficult. I'm a bit of a chatterbox and now I was not able to say a single word for three weeks . . . If I wanted to communicate, I had to use a notepad and pen. The English papers were also full of rumors that I had gotten fat. Ordinarily, I wouldn't have cared all that much, but things were tough enough as they were. I'll never forget something that happened one of those days, as I walked past a couple of blokes on the street. One of them turned to the other and said, "Wasn't that Sam Fox?"

"Nah, can't have been, she's fat now."

I bit my lip and tried to focus on everything else that I hadn't had time for lately, like finding a new home for my monkey, Norman. He was a silvery marmoset I had been given for my twenty-first birthday, and he lived in a big cage. I used to let him have free run of the house all the same, because I didn't like keeping him locked up. Back when Dad was living with us, he hated it, because Norman would pee on all of his antiques and on the curtains and lampshades. I actually liked Norman's lack of respect, not least because I could sometimes use it to my advantage. For example, if a journalist had come over to interview me and I decided I didn't like him or her, or just wanted the interview to end, I would invite that person to scratch Norman's belly. It wasn't exactly hard to get people to do it, because everyone thought he was so sweet. But almost immediately, Norman's willy would be sticking out, and then a golden stream of liquid would squirt at the interviewer with full force.

Sadly, I didn't have the time to take care of Norman properly, but I managed to find a solution to the problem during those three weeks. There was a local taxi firm that I often used, and when Mum explained the situation to them, they welcomed Norman with open arms. That way, he never had to be left on his own, because there were always people in the taxi office.

Before I knew it, those three torturous weeks of silence were over. I remember feeling extremely nervous before going back to the doctor. I was about to learn whether I would be forced to shelve my music career, or whether I could start hoping for a way back. Thankfully, as the doctor started to examine me, I quickly realized that the operation must have been a success. Next thing I knew, he had confirmed it with those three magic words, "Everything looks fine."

It was April by the time I finally went back to New York to record the video for "Naughty Girls Need Love Too."

Since we needed a group of male dancers for the video, we held auditions at a dance school in Manhattan in the days leading up to the shoot. The auditions were my idea, and the jury consisted of me, Mum, and the director, Scott Kalvert. Scott was a real newbie back then—the only thing he had really worked on was Taylor Dayne's "Tell It To My Heart." Going forward, he would make music video after music video for artists like Cyndi Lauper, the Fresh Prince (a.k.a. Will Smith), and Bobby Brown. He even went on to make a couple of really successful films in the nineties before tragically taking his own life in 2014.

In any case, we were sitting on plastic chairs behind a desk in that dance school, waiting for the first man to do his thing. Since none of them had heard the song before, we let them go into the room next door to practice. Then they came back out and showed us their dance. To finish things off, they would take off their tops for a Polaroid. It was a lot of fun, particularly for me, because it felt like the tables had been turned. I remember shouting, "Your top! Don't forget your top!" and then "Next!" We had similar auditions for the "I Wanna Have Some Fun" video, too, and when it came to the shoot for "Hurt Me, Hurt Me (But the Pants Stay On)," we had auditions for both men and women. One of the girls I chose was Jennifer Lopez; you can see her in the video. I thought she was fantastic. Even though she was unknown at that point, you could see that there was something special about her. While the other girls chatted away to one another during rehearsals, she kept to herself. She also brought her own lunch with her and was incredibly focused and dedicated—incredibly beautiful too, of course. Some female artists struggle with picking beautiful women as dancers or background singers because it makes them feel insecure, but I wanted everyone in my videos to be beautiful. The minute I saw Jennifer Lopez, I said, "That girl looks fantastic, we have to have her!"

We shot the video for "I Wanna Have Some Fun" in Central Park, and "Naughty Girls" was filmed on a basketball court somewhere; I've forgotten exactly where. But that evening, we all went out in the Meatpacking District. It was me, the producers Full Force, and all of the men we'd found during the auditions.

Ahead of the shoot, Scott and I had talked for quite some time about what we could do with my image, a conversation that led to me dyeing my hair pink—something several other female artists would copy going forward. When it came to clothing, I wore my ripped jeans and a leather jacket covered in patches that I'd collected from all over the world while I was modeling. The stylist who helped me was Patricia Field, who later went on to work on *Sex and the City*. She was the one responsible for making my rocky style seem more feminine and sexy. Among other things, she pulled out a white top and a really nice sombrero cordobés.

Music videos take a lot of time to make—which can be really irritating for a restless person like me. That particular video took an extra long time because we were shooting in several different locations. On top of the outdoor scenes, we also did a studio shoot. Back then, MTV used to show different versions of music videos at night, so while we were filming, we made sure to shoot some extra, sexy scenes for use in the night version. Mum was standing only a few yards away from me, which made it difficult to relax, especially when it came to my scene with the guy who played the lead role in the video. Richard looked great and worked at one of New York's hottest strip clubs—Chippendales. As we were filming, I heard Mum say, loudly and clearly, "I can hardly believe my daughter is doing this."

We shot the video for "I Wanna Have Some Fun" with Scott later that year. I wasn't so keen on my counterpart's looks that time. Compared to Richard, his looks were almost cheesy, which made everything harder. I just didn't feel the same chemistry with him. With Richard, things had felt charged, and I knew he had felt it, too. Shooting those sexy scenes, he'd had an erection practically the whole time.

When "Naughty Girls" was eventually sent out to radio stations, it quickly got quite a few plays on the more urban shows, and the video was often on MTV. But what really kicked things off for the track was a twelve-inch featuring a remix of the song that was sent to discos and clubs across the US. No one knew it was me singing on the track, and my name didn't appear anywhere on it. All it said on the cover of the record was, "Play it again, Sam."

In any case, by June 1988, "Naughty Girls" had reached number three on the *Billboard* charts, and the single "I Wanna Have Some Fun," which was released a month or so later, made it to number eight. It meant that I'd had three top ten hits in the US in the space of just one year. And with "Naughty Girls," I was also the first white artist to top the black dance music and general dance charts.

But though I'd proven myself as an artist, the papers—or the British ones, at least—couldn't stop writing about my breasts. For the whole of that spring in 1988, they were obsessed with the idea that they had gotten smaller. There were headlines like, "Sam's Lost 4in from Her Bust!" It really was tiring, especially when I returned to London to do more PR work immediately after ending a PR tour of the US. I was burned out, and looking back, I don't know how I had the energy or the time to do it all. I could be in the studio recording jingles for forty-three radio stations for a couple of hours, then have to rush over to Radio 1 for an interview, simultaneously being followed by one or more journalists doing a piece on "A Day in the Life of Samantha Fox." And on top of all that, I also had to try to make my relationship with Paul work.

In a way, it was like we had some kind of unspoken agreement. You could probably say that we made use of one another, that we were friends with benefits. We were both equally aware of it, but it wasn't something we ever actually talked about. It didn't feel like there was any real reason to bring it up. He knew I didn't love him, and I knew he didn't love me. But we had fun, and got lots out of our time together. If I saw him today, it would feel completely relaxed—despite the fact that neither of us was faithful during our relationship. I mean, sometimes, when I stayed over at his place and he left for the studio, I would hear other girls leaving messages on his answering machine. And, for my part, it was around this time that I started a love affair with Jive's international manager.

Since she's married with a family now, I'll call her Kat. If I'm completely honest, I don't actually think she was gay. She had never been with another woman before me, and she probably hasn't been since. But I had always been attracted to women, ever since I was small; I got my first girlfriend when I was only seven. Her name was Donna and we used to play doctors in the Wendy house at home. I was always the doctor and she was the nurse. Later, I had a huge crush on Lindsay Wagner, the actress, and could hardly wait until Friday came round, when I would get to see her on TV. I was also in love with two of the teachers at school. Not that any of this was something I ever talked about—and since I was a virgin when I broke through as a model, I wasn't really clear about my sexuality. It all felt very confusing. I was so young that it was hard to know what was what. But despite that, Mum understood. Years later, when we finally talked about it, she just said, "I knew all along, Sammy. I knew all along."

By the time I finally worked it out for myself, I remember being scared—scared of what people would say, because I had so many male fans. And since I did sometimes get with girls, rumors about my sexual orientation started up early on in my career. There were always journalists calling up to ask whether I was with this person or that, but I always denied it. I honestly didn't dare do anything else. I mean, I was a former pinup girl and had absolutely no way of knowing how the truth would go down.

Anyway, Kat was the first woman I had a serious relationship with. She even moved in with me. Looking back now, I can't understand how we never got found out.

As I mentioned before, I was going crazy with all the time differences. I mean, in any given week I might spend two days in New York, two in London, and then three in LA. I was constantly jet-lagged, and so, one day in late summer 1988, I called Steven at Jive and said, "If you want me to keep selling records in the US, you need to fix it so I can live there. I can't be doing PR all across the country and live in London at the same time."

It was true. To stay at the top in the US, you really did need to be there. People tend to forget just how big it is; every state is practically a country in its own right. It can take four months just to promote one album. But that was hardly the only reason I did everything I could to convince Steven to pay for accommodation for me in New York. It was only once he said that I had a point and I realized he was on my side that I added, "But I don't want to live alone."

Stephen didn't seem to understand a thing. "No?"

"It would be lonely. Even the thought of it scares me."

"Aha."

"I want Kat to come with me."

The whole thing was the plan Kat and I had cooked up, of course, and probably our only chance of being able to live together.

In any case, Steven promised to ask Kat what she thought of my idea, and when he called her a few days later, she played along.

Everyone knew we worked well together and that we were tight. Plus, both Kat and I had boyfriends, so none of what I was proposing seemed in any way odd. Not even my closest friends suspected anything, which meant we were able to avoid a load of coverage in the press. What did happen, however, was that the English papers made a big deal of the move. They wrote that I was leaving Britain for the USA, that I was turning my back on my country, and so on. But I had always thought of Britain as my home, not least because that was where my family and friends were. It made sense to keep promoting my work in the US, because not as many people from England have made it in America as you might think. Robbie Williams does live in the US, but that's mostly because he can't stand the fame in Europe and preferred a country where he was less well-known. Not even Kylie (Minogue) managed to make it in the States to begin with. Back then, it was basically just Annie Lennox and I who had an audience there. And I think I'm still the only female artist to have had three top ten hits simultaneously on both sides of the Atlantic. There's a Trivial Pursuit question that asks which of a selection of British artists (Samantha Fox, Annie Lennox, and a couple of other singers) have managed it. Everyone guesses Annie Lennox, of course, but it's me!

Early that autumn, Kat flew to New York to look for an apartment for us. I had told her I didn't want some kind of modern, minimalist home; I wanted something more homely. Since I spent so much of my time in hotels, I'd started hating minimalism. I didn't want to live on the Upper West Side, either. It felt far too posh. Back in the early days, I'd spent a lot of time in that part of the city, because it made a good base for doing promo work, but I had never felt comfortable there. And not just because of the type of people who lived there; it was also because it was a pretty lively area. At the time, New York could be quiet and calm on one street, and swarming with crack addicts and slums just around the corner.

I wanted to find something that reminded me of my neighborhood back home in London. Kat worked flat out, faxing over pictures of a number of different apartments. Eventually, she managed to find a very nice place on Eleventh Street, between Fifth and Broadway. It was being rented out by a playwright, and she'd decorated in what I'd call a bohemian style, with lots of stripped floorboards, rugs, cushions, huge sofas, and an open fireplace. There was an en suite bathroom and a walk-in wardrobe, and Kat had her own bedroom (for the sake of appearances).

When I went to see the apartment two weeks later, I liked it immediately—it was actually even nicer than it looked in the pictures. Being able to feel the energy a place has, and see how it smells, is a very different experience.

"It's so nice!" I said as Kat showed me round.

"I know! Just wait 'til you see the neighborhood," she smiled.

I understood what she meant when we went out a little later. The building wasn't far from the famous Chelsea Hotel, and the entire area was cool and trendy, full of shoe shops and bars. It was early autumn at the time, which is the prettiest season in New York, and that particular day felt especially beautiful. The sunlight fell between the buildings as we walked, and the air felt unusually crisp and clean. Kat pointed things out and explained where everything was. There was a gay area nearby, for example, Christopher Street, which was full of cafés and really did remind me of Camden Town in London.

It didn't take long for Kat and me to find our feet, not just in the apartment and the neighborhood, but in the city itself.

As I mentioned before, I've never had all that many female friends. Maybe it's partly down to girls feeling threatened by me and preferring to keep their distance. And once I became famous, it was like they always had a predetermined notion of who I was. The worst example might be from a few years earlier, when I travelled to Cyprus to open a hotel. The hotel's PR man and his wife were with me the entire time, and I had noticed that there was something tense and slightly forced about the woman. I later heard that she had nearly had a breakdown at the thought of me being alone in a room with her husband. Like I would have wanted *him*. I mean, the man was short, fat, and bald.

Anyway, all that changed in New York, largely as a result of me meeting a handful of incredible women, among them Celeste and Natalie. Both were fans of mine, and they used to wait outside the radio stations whenever I was being interviewed. They would also call up the radio shows like madwomen to request my songs. So, when I spotted Celeste at one of my record signings in the city, I made sure she could come and sit next to me for the whole thing. She and Nathalie were younger than me, but we became friends all the same. They showed me New York and took me out to a whole load of cool clubs and bars.

Those really were good times. Yes, there were moments when Kat and I clashed, often because of her jealousy. But I also felt more relaxed and free than I had in a long time. When I was with a woman, it was almost as though I didn't have to step into the role of Samantha Fox, either in bed or in my everyday life. Being myself was enough.

16

BRIT AWARDS

I was about to introduce the Four Tops, the legendary soul group, so I raised an arm and said, "Ladies and gentlemen, the Four Tops!" Only, Boy George walked out onto the stage instead.

I began 1989 by hosting the Brit Awards, a huge awards ceremony organized by the record industry. Since I was so busy in the US, I had initially turned it down, but the organizers were so keen to have me that they offered to fly me over the Atlantic on the Concorde. It was flattering, of course—even the fact they had asked if I wanted to host the ceremony seemed like recognition to me.

But no matter how we twist and turn the matter, there are only twenty-four hours in a day, and when I landed at Heathrow I was exhausted. The next day, when I got to the Royal Albert Hall for rehearsals ahead of the event that night, I was also suffering from terrible jet lag. For some reason, I still didn't feel all that nervous, and the rehearsals, which took no more than four hours, also went well.

It was only that evening that everything started to go to pot.

I would be hosting the ceremony alongside Mick Fleetwood. His band, Fleetwood Mac, had long been one of my favorites, and I was particularly in awe of Stevie Nicks. In fact, I had always hoped I would get to meet her one day, so I could tell her how fantastic I thought she was.

In any case, I was in my dressing room, feeling slightly nervous at the thought of soon stepping out onto the stage with Mick in front of the entire music and record industry, when the BBC stylist came in to iron our outfits—fitted black tuxedos with sequined arms.

Suddenly, I saw something drop out of Mick's jacket pocket and land on the floor with a thud. It was a huge, triangle-shaped lump of hash.

"What was that?" The stylist had heard the sound and was now looking down at the floor.

I quickly kicked the lump of hash beneath the door, where it got wedged in the gap.

"Uh . . . oh look, it's a doorstop!" I said, struggling to hide my relief at being able to come up with something so quickly.

For a moment, the stylist gave me a skeptical look, but then she seemed to decide not to dig any deeper and just laid Mick's jacket on the ironing board to start ironing. I breathed out. I mean, I didn't want Mick to get into trouble. We had enough to worry about as it was.

I decided to go over to his dressing room to say hello and see what was going on.

"Come in," a voice growled as I knocked on his door. As I pushed it open, the sight that greeted me instantly set me on edge.

Mick was slumped lazily in a worn-out old armchair, puffing on an enormous joint. He was surrounded by a huge cloud of pine-scented smoke.

"Hello," he said with a good-natured smile, slowly getting up to greet me.

It was only then that I saw how incredibly tall he was.

"Good luck," I said, having to stand on my tiptoes to give him a kiss on the cheek.

"Same," Mick smiled, looking like he was about to topple forward onto me as he leaned down. His beard also smelled strongly of hash.

As I hurried back to my dressing room to touch up my makeup, it was no longer my own performance on stage that worried me.

And things didn't get any better when, not long afterwards, I went back to Mick's room and shouted through the door, "You ready, Mick?" There was no answer.

I waited a moment, then shouted again, but all I got in return was silence. So I gently opened the door and stepped inside.

Mick was sitting in the same position as earlier, in the same armchair. But he was wearing his jacket now, and was puffing on another big, fat joint.

By that point, I was incredibly nervous and didn't know quite what to say.

"I can just feel that it's going to be a great night!" I eventually managed, in an attempt to get a single sign of life out of him.

But Mick just stared at me with empty eyes, and I wondered, in confusion, how this was going to work. In that kind of context, you really do need a reliable sidekick, someone to hold your hand. I had some experience from my time presenting *The Six O'Clock Show* and as a VJ on MTV, but that's a world away from hosting a live broadcast of an awards ceremony that half of Britain will be watching.

Mick and I had barely made it on stage before everything started to go wrong. Through my earpiece, I could hear the backstage team frantically searching for people who weren't in position. There were also crowds of Bros fans right by the stage, screaming so loudly and constantly that the old lady looking after the Autocue in front of us couldn't hear what we were saying and therefore had no idea where in the script we were. That, in turn, meant I occasionally had no idea what I was meant to be saying, since the text on the screen was either too early or too late. But if I turned to Mick for help, it was like looking into a big, empty house. The lights were on but no one was home.

Everything that could go wrong really did go wrong. I mean, I was about to introduce the Four Tops, the legendary soul group, so I raised an arm and said, "Ladies and gntlemen, the Four Tops!" Only, Boy George walked out onto the stage instead. I could hear someone shouting in my ear, "No, no, that's not the Four Tops!

That's Boy George!" which I could obviously see for myself. I had known Boy George for a while. I'd met him, among other places, at a photography studio when I was eighteen, and he had invited himself over for tea with my family, then somehow got lost en route on the day we had chosen.

In any case, he quickly said, "I'm the one top. The Four Tops are being held up—they're putting their makeup on."

I was so embarrassed I wanted to die, or at least be swallowed up by the stage floor. I turned to Mick again, but he was away with the fairies. On top of all that, the Bros fan club were continuing their non-stop screeching by my feet, and one of the girls kept shouting out, "Slag!" to me. It drove me mad, and when it was finally time for an ad break, my polished facade came crashing down—only to be replaced by the East End girl in me. I bent down and grabbed the girl's shirt collar.

"If you don't shut up, I'll bash you!" I shouted.

It pained me that there were so many huge stars there that night, both in the audience and on stage. Ordinarily, I would have thought it was great to meet my idols, but on that particular night it felt like more of a nightmare that they were witnessing the fiasco, along with half of the British population—though I wasn't actually responsible for any of it.

One person who did seem to feel sorry for me was Joe Elliott. Just as he and the rest of Def Leppard were about to go on stage to perform, he put an arm around my shoulders and said, "You all right, luv?"

As they played their song, I waited right behind the backdrop, and all I wanted was to avoid going back out on stage—something I told Joe once they were finished. He looked me straight in the eye and said, "It's not your fault it ended up like this. The whole thing's a mess." He nodded towards an assistant who was running in our direction with a wild look in her eye. "No one seems to know what's going on."

His thoughtfulness and calm reminded me of why I had always preferred rock bands to pop stars: they just weren't anywhere near as pretentious or self-obsessed.

For obvious reasons, having to go to the after-party later that night didn't feel especially good. I felt like people were looking at me and convinced myself they were also laughing behind my back. But just as I stood there, feeling terrible, trying to keep up a conversation with Mick Fleetwood and Keith Richards, the very thing I had been dreaming about for so long finally happened: I caught sight of Stevie Nicks, and realized she was heading straight towards me! Of course, it wasn't me she had spotted in the crowd; it was Mick. She grabbed hold of his arm and slurred something I couldn't make out.

Mick politely introduced me to her, but she just stared at me like I was more or less nothing but air.

After a long moment, she said something I couldn't catch and then turned back to Mick and practically clung to his arm. It's probably fair to say that she wasn't having one of her better days, and I didn't feel particularly offended, just a little sad that this was often how it turned out when I met my idols.

I slept terribly that night, and, as expected, the slating started the very next day. The journalists wanted to make the fiasco my fault, and they called me things like an empty-headed bimbo. The British press like nothing more than building you up just to knock you down again. It was inevitable that my love affair with the English would end at some point, and it happened with a vengeance after the Brits.

All the same, I didn't have the time either to think about it or to dwell on what had happened, because I was booked to play the Sanremo Music Festival just a few days later. Almost immediately after that, I was due to fly back to the US for a longer signing tour.

I was doing so much promo work at the time that everything has kind of merged together in my mind, but I'll never forget signing records at one of LA's biggest record stores during that particular tour. There were crowds of people like always, but things were still fairly calm and ordered, or at least they were until a sudden—and, to me, inexplicable—commotion started up over by the entrance. A minute or two later, I saw a group of big black men (some wearing suits, others dressed more casually) walking straight past the queue. To begin with, it surprised me that no one was protesting, but soon I understood why. I watched as a man peeled away from the group of beefcakes and stepped towards me with one of my latest records in his hand. It was only then that I realized who it was—Mike Tyson.

"Hi," he said with what almost looked like a shy smile.

"Hello," I replied.

"Could I get your autograph?"

"Of course," I smiled, hurrying to write my name on the cover as the camera flashes went off.

"I was passing by and saw you were here," Mike continued, "so I thought I would see if you wanted to come to the fight tomorrow. I'm fighting Frank Bruno in Vegas."

"Yeah, I saw," I said, which was true; there were posters for the title fight everywhere. The only problem was that I also had a full working schedule for the day. That was what I told Mike, who smiled that shy smile of his, which didn't tally at all with the rest of his appearance. He said, "If I send you a private plane, would you come and watch?"

I didn't know what to say. I mean, Frank Bruno was a hero back in England, so obviously I wondered what people back there would say if they spotted me sitting in Mike's gang by the ringside. But at the same time, I really did like the sport and had gone to several fights with Dad when I was younger. So, after sitting in silence for a second or two too long, I said, "Yeah."

"Great! See you then," Mike said, turning and leaving the shop with my record in his hand and his posse behind him.

Just as Mike had promised, he sent his private plane for me, and as I sat in the taxi on the way to the fight in the Las Vegas Hilton, I felt really excited—and continued that way, at least until the fight itself got started.

The two men really let loose on one another, and when you're sitting that close to the ring, you can hear every single blow and see how they're really hurting one another, bit by bit. If I'm completely honest, I thought parts of it were pretty disgusting. But at the same time, I couldn't stop looking.

Suddenly, Mike knocked Frank Bruno to the floor with a right hook, and the entire arena roared in unison. But Bruno got back onto all fours, and towards the end of the first round, he managed a left-right combination that shook Mike.

I was so excited that I completely forgot myself and shouted, "Yeah!"

Tyson's entire gang turned to stare at me. A few of them might have thought I just didn't understand boxing at all, but one person who continued glaring was Mike's girlfriend, the supermodel Naomi Campbell.

Mike eventually started to dominate in the ring, and by the end of the fifth round, he won on a technical knockout. Everything was fine then, and the after-party was just as everyone—everyone in Tyson's gang, that is—had hoped. I noticed Mike looking over at me a couple of times, but Naomi was keeping an eagle eye on both me and him, so I barely dared glance in his direction.

Not long after that, I flew back to England to take part in a couple of TV programs, and I took the opportunity to go out for lunch with my friend Jonathan King.

Jonathan had started out as a pop artist in the sixties, going on to have several big hits before starting his own record label, to which he signed bands like Genesis and 10cc. He really did know everything about the music industry, and he'd given me a lot of good advice. On top of that, he was a great listener and easy to talk to, which was actually the main reason I had arranged to meet him at a pub in Islington. Dad had started drinking more and more lately, and he was practically always either drunk or high whenever we went away with work. It worried me, because it felt like he wasn't in control of anything anymore, not least my career. That's what I told Jonathan after our food arrived.

He nodded gravely, sat in silence for a moment, and then said, "It was good for you to have your dad managing you here in England while it was mostly modeling jobs; he didn't have to do much other than pick up the phone when it rang. He never had to call around actually selling you to people. But now that you're working all over the world, it's a whole new ball game."

Jonathan told me that he knew someone in the US who worked as both lawyer and manager for Whitney Houston, Eric Clapton, Elton John, and others.

"That's the kind of bloke you need, Sam."

"Definitely," I said. 'But how do you suggest I explain that to Dad?"

Jonathan swallowed a mouthful of food and then smiled.

"You don't have to. I'll write him a letter and explain how I see the situation. If he wants the best for you, he'll realize I'm right."

Jonathan kept his word and sent that letter.

But rather than thanking him when he read it a few days later, Dad reacted just as I had feared.

"Who the hell does he think he is?!" he shouted, waving the piece of paper in my face as we sat in his house in Crouch End.

"But Dad," I tried, "he means well, and it probably would be good to have a lawyer as my manager in the US. It makes it easier to keep on top of the record label there and make sure they're paying all the royalties they're meant to, and that the sales of merch and other things are really working."

"I look after all that!" Dad hissed, tearing the letter to shreds before my eyes. "That piece of shit isn't going to tell me what to do or how to do it."

In that moment, I realized that Dad would never voluntarily let go of me and my affairs. What I didn't understand back then was the real reason behind it; I thought it was just because he was fairly controlling in nature.

The next evening, I invited Jonathan out for dinner at one of his favorite restaurants, La Gavroche.

"I really love coming here; the waiters are so handsome," he grinned, casting an appreciative glance at a young, male waiter who was passing by. "So, what did your dad think of my idea?"

I sighed and told him exactly what had happened. To my surprise, Jonathan didn't seem the least bit offended. Instead, he looked at me thoughtfully for a moment and then said, "Hmm . . . I have another good friend I could ask—Sharon Osbourne. I'm sure I could get her to be your manager."

I really liked the idea, because I liked her. But I also realized that Dad would refuse any suggestions that I, Jonathan, or anyone else made. And so I mumbled something like, "Yeah, even Dad should be able to see how good that would be."

"Yeah, he really should," Jonathan said, raising his wine glass with a smile. "But now I think it's time for a toast, because you'll be off on the road soon."

I was more than happy to toast to that, because ever since it had been decided that I would head out on my first real tour that spring, I'd felt an excitement that at times was almost unbearable. I would finally get to stand on stage with a band behind me, and I'd get to do it in huge arenas in countries like the US, Canada, Costa Rica, Colombia, Bolivia, Argentina, Japan, South Korea, Malaysia, and so on. It had also just been confirmed that New Kids on the Block would be the support act for some of the tour. I told Jonathan, whose face lit up when he said, "Then we need to go and see them when I'm in New York next week. I know they're playing Yankee Stadium then."

Jonathan had an apartment in New York, and by the very next week, he had fixed us some tickets to that show. Neither of us really had any idea what was awaiting us as we took a taxi to Yankee Stadium, which turned out to be full of teenage girls who started screaming even before the boys walked on stage. And when Donnie

Wahlberg and the others eventually appeared, the girls started screaming so loudly that I had to cover my ears. New Kids on the Block were the first real boy band, so I had never experienced anything like it, and I was quite shocked to see that people in the crowd were actually throwing up with excitement.

Suddenly, Jonathan tapped me on the shoulder and shouted in my ear, "I can't bear any more of this!"

He hurried out of the arena. I sat there a while longer, trying to get used to the idea that I would be experiencing this same kind of madness on many evenings to come over the next six months.

17

DO YOU WANT TO HAVE SOME FUN— WORLD TOUR

In the mornings, when I woke up and stepped out of my little suite at the very back of the bus, I literally almost fainted at the stink of the boys in the band. They had the same porn film on repeat on the TV, and the mess I had to work my way through was indescribable.

The light, the air, the sounds—everything is so clear when I think back to that morning in early May when I stood on the street outside the building where Kat and I lived, waiting for my band to pick me up. New York had just woken up and the streets were bustling, but I was filled with the kind of calm you only experience when all the pieces fall into place. The six-month world tour I was about to embark on was, in my eyes, my reward for years of hard work.

Kat was up in the apartment, bringing down the last of our bags. I had just put on my sunglasses and lit a cigarette when I heard a familiar voice.

"Hey there!"

It was Paul, who had come over to say goodbye and to wish me luck. We had been seeing one another more and more sporadically over the last six months, and by the time I saw him coming towards me that morning with a big smile on his face, he had smoothly transitioned from being a boyfriend into a good friend.

"How's it feel?" he asked, giving me a hug.

"Fantastic," I replied, spotting the tour bus approaching over his shoulder. "And here's the band!"

Paul turned around and exclaimed, "Wow, you've got the Guns N' Roses tour bus. That's cool!"

The bus was pretty garish, pink and blue with a huge palm tree painted on one side. I saw one of my backing singers, Catherine, waving to me through a window, and the minute the bus stopped, John Durno jumped out onto the pavement and shouted, "Ready?"

Yes, I was ready, and even after we had driven all the way to the Deep South and reached our first venue—an enormous basketball arena in Alabama—I was so excited I had barely even noticed the long journey.

We had spent the past three months rehearsing in New York. Back then, the preparations were much more comprehensive; nothing was computerized, and we had six different synths, each of which needed programming individually. Those early samplers were nothing like the equipment that's available today.

In any case, the first gig gave me a real kick, despite the fact that I got some criticism afterwards. Jonathan King had flown down to see me, and after the show he took me to one side in my dressing room and said, "Try not to stand with your back to the crowd, Sam. You need to show more self-confidence and look people in the eye. And don't forget the people at the very back; they always get ignored."

Since I paid my musicians on a weekly basis and the arena gigs usually took place at weekends, we had arranged to play club gigs on weeknights. It goes without saying that those gigs were completely different to the arena shows, but I liked both, and as the tour went on, I really did start to enjoy everything. I felt safe on stage with my band, even if the drummer did make me slightly nervous.

The first synth drums from a brand called Simmons had just come out, and my drummer was obsessed with walking around, recording different sounds on his DAT recorder all day. Then, later, as I was dancing to different rhythms on stage, I might suddenly hear, "OH YEAH! OH YEAH! COME ON! COME ON!" Or he would play an abrupt crazed laugh, or some other strange sound would come booming out of the speakers. To begin with, I had no idea where it was coming from.

Every night, the drummer would come up with some new sound—each one stranger than the last—which he had decided to add to the track, worsening rather than improving it.

Jesus Christ, I thought, casting him angry glances. I wanted a solid drummer, someone who could groove even if he was just playing a straight beat, not some idiot introducing a load of new sounds and wrecking the choreography we had spent weeks perfecting.

Just a few gigs into the tour, I realized I needed to replace him with a new drummer. I asked my tour manager, Glenn, who had previously run tours for people like Steve Marriott, to fly in a couple of men to audition. One of them was a typical rock drummer and I decided to take him with us immediately on hearing him play.

But after two or three gigs, I realized he was too rock 'n' roll. Yes, he could keep to a beat, but it was like he had no groove; he just banged away. It also meant that he didn't manage the dance sections of the show, where we needed a dynamic that he just didn't have. On top of that, he insisted on playing double bass drums, which didn't really work with my songs. So we replaced him with a third drummer, who unfortunately also turned out to be completely useless.

As I tried to make him understand how I wanted him to play, forcing myself to be as patient as possible, he said—in a slightly affronted tone—"I never had this kind of problem when I played with La Toya Jackson."

In total, I would end up working with four different drummers on that tour.

But, as luck would have it, I didn't have the same problems with the rest of the band. My guitarist, Nunzio, was a fantastic musician and had previously toured with artists like Rod Stewart. He also had a great body with pretty big muscles, which meant that the girls loved him. The interest was mutual, and Nunzio used to scratch his phone number into the plectrums taped to his mic stand and then throw them to girls he'd spotted in the crowd. He had a really nice girlfriend back in New York, but that never stopped him from taking some extra time in his dressing room at the end of the night—while the rest of us were already in the bus, waiting to leave.

By this point, AIDS had become a big deal, and I did spend quite a lot of time worrying—not just about Nunzio, but about all the men in the band, and I started putting condoms in their pay packets. In a way, I felt responsible for them. Other than my bassist, the MD, John Durno, and the keyboard player, who was a good guy, I didn't really trust any of them. I would let them have one beer ahead of every show, but no more. I personally never drank anything before a gig, and I was very strict on that point. After the gig, the guys could have a couple more beers to wind down—but not if we had another show the next day. If I saw them drinking more than I allowed, they would be given a warning.

I was completely against drugs and told them, "If I find out you're taking drugs, you're out."

I knew all too well what happened when several members of a band were on drugs. There would be an immediate segregation between them and the others. I wanted us to work as a close-knit team, because only then would we be able to achieve my vision of how we should sound and appear on stage. If there was a bad apple among the members, it would ruin everything we were striving for.

Something else I learned during this tour was that you should never allow girlfriends on the road with you, purely because it meant that jealousy and arguments cropped up far too easily. Plus, it changed the entire mood of everyone in the band. On one occasion, when we were somewhere in the Deep South, I remember that we arrived at a Hilton late at night, and that Glenn's wife was waiting for us there. She greeted me guardedly after hearing Glenn shout to me, "Come on, babe, grab your bag!"

He always called me "babe," and none of us thought anything more of it. But it turned out that his room was next to mine, and as I lay in bed trying to get to sleep, I could hear Glenn's wife screaming at him through the wall, accusing him of having an affair with me.

I groaned into my pillow, because I realized they would keep me awake all night. All the same, I was relieved to escape the dorm-room feeling I got when we slept on the bus. In the mornings, when I woke up and stepped out of my little suite at the very back of the bus, I literally almost fainted at the stink of the boys in the band. They had the same porn film on repeat on the TV, and the mess I had to work my way through was indescribable.

After three weeks of touring, we made it to Disney World in Orlando, Florida, where we were due to play a number of gigs with New Kids on the Block and EMF as support acts. Every evening, I would do three forty-five-minutes shows on a huge stage outside Cinderella's Castle, and it felt really good to be working in one place for a while—though we actually came close to not being able to perform there at all. It turned out that some worrying rumors had reached Disney, who phoned up Dad for reassurances that I wasn't the porn star Samantha Fox. It wasn't the first time I had been confused with her, and every time it happened, it upset me just as much. Especially after I saw one of her films and realized that she was much older than me and had a droopy, spotty arse.

In any case, the gigs at Disney World went well, even if we did run into some practical difficulties. My changing room was at the very top of Cinderella's Castle, where the lift didn't always work, meaning that my assistant, Paula, had to run up all the stairs to grab the hair dryer and fresh clothes for the next show. I only had half an hour between performances to fix my hair, change my clothes, drink some tea, rest my voice, etc. So when Paula made it back downstairs with everything I needed, out of breath and drenched in sweat, she didn't even have time to rest. Instead, she had to rush to fix my makeup and help me into my new clothes. Then it was time to head back out on stage. Paula also made sure to tie a scarf around my neck and to wrap me up in a robe after every show, to keep me warm. She made sure I didn't chat too much, and kept the journalists and other people at a distance, so that I could warm down my voice in peace and quiet. She was really smart and would be by my side for ten years, until she got married and had kids.

Once the gigs in Orlando were over, we were scheduled for a number of performances at Disneyland in Anaheim, California. But before that, we were making a quick trip to Costa Rica, which turned out to be just the first in a line of problems and plenty of indescribable suffering on my part.

We reached our hotel sometime in the middle of the night. The first thing we saw was a huge, illuminated, turquoise pool—and since we were so hot and sweaty from the long journey, we jumped straight in with our clothes on.

The next day, we discovered how beautiful the Pacific coast was, and suddenly it felt extremely luxurious that we would be able to spend a few free days at the hotel after our show that evening.

"We're spending all day on the beach tomorrow!" John said, casting a happy glance out to sea before we climbed into the minibus to head to the arena for sound check.

The next day, we made the very most of the sun. When lunchtime came around, I went up to the little beach café and ate a burger before returning to the crystal-clear, seventy-five-degree water.

But the next morning, I woke feeling more unwell than I had ever felt before. I rushed out to the toilet and barely had time to sit down before it felt like my stomach had turned itself inside out. I spent the whole day throwing up and didn't feel even remotely better by the next day, when we were due to fly back to the US.

With Myra in Canada on a PR job for my album *Angel with an Attitude*.

On the way from Marbella to Seville to see my then-boyfriend Rafi Camino perform during a bullfight, with my friends from New York, Natalie, *left*, and Celeste, *right*, plus my bodyguard—and Mum's then boyfriend—Colin, *second from left*, and my neighbors in Spain, Geoff and Sue.

Nan and Grandad celebrating their golden wedding anniversary and holding up a picture of one of the first times they met.

With Nan out behind the house on Truro Road, where I lived after Dad cheated me out of my money.

With my friends before we board Rafi Camino's plane, which will take us to the bullfight in Seville.

Wearing a Soviet officer's hat, with the Winter Palace in Saint Petersburg in the background.

Photo shoot for my first calendar, in the Spanish village of Mijas on the Costa del Sol.

In Kiev for a gig with Lorraine McIntosh, *left,* and Chrissie.

I stole the limelight from Sabrina at Ku Club in Ibiza by diving into the pool from the stage just before she performed on the live Italian TV show.

In Beirut during my Middle East tour, 1995.

I won Page Three Girl of the Year for the second year in a row and celebrated it at Stringfellows in London, with the comedian Bobby Davro, among others.

Charity tennis tour for children's hospitals in Ecuador. Here, I'm with the rock star Rick Springfield, *left*, Dirk Benedict from the A Team, *middle*, and Colin.

Release party for the *Touch Me* album in New York. My entire family is there, and it's Vanessa's first time in the US.

Interviewing Vanessa on *The Six O'Clock Show*. The segment is called "Sisters."

With Paula, *left*, and Myra at a festival in Germany, 2004. Myra played keyboard and Paula bass.

Vanessa and me ahead of a PR tour for "Nothing's Gonna Stop Me Now," 1987.

Me as a brunette when I went to church.

With Arsenal's A
team. My boyfriend
Kenny Sansom is at
the far right.

As a result, the flight was a nightmare journey where I filled one sick bag after another, despite having eaten barely anything—all I'd had were a few sips of water and Coca-Cola, in an attempt to avoid becoming completely dehydrated. I stepped off the plane on shaking legs and still felt very weak that evening, when I walked out on stage at Disneyland, in front of another huge and enthusiastic crowd. My nausea had reached a point beyond all description, and I had made sure there was a bucket right behind the stage.

Against all odds, I managed to complete the main part of the show, but as I reached the halfway point of "Do Ya Do Ya (Wanna Please Me)," our first encore song, I ran over to the drummer and shouted, "Drum solo . . . Do a drum solo!"

Shortly after that, I was off the stage. I pulled down my jeans and squatted over the bucket. It was coming out of both ends at the same time, and when John came over to see how I was doing, his eyes widened and he stepped back in embarrassment.

I had no choice but to pull my jeans back up and run straight out onto the stage to finish the song. Despite the fact I could barely stand, I even managed the final encore track, "Touch Me," and once that was over I collapsed into a chair in my dressing room. There were two main reasons I wanted to finish the show no matter what. The first was that I didn't want to let down all of the people who had come to see me, who might even have traveled a long way. The second was that I had fought so long and so hard to even make it onto that stage that I didn't want to let anything as banal as a stomach bug stop me.

But after the gig, I went to a local hospital, where they gave me an x-ray and discovered that I had a parasite in my stomach. The doctor showed me the x-ray, and though I felt completely awful, I screamed when I saw what looked like a big, white beetle with eight legs that had wedged itself in my intestine. It was like something from a horror movie.

In any case, I was prescribed tablets to kill the monster, and thanks to those, I managed to make it through the remaining shows at Disneyland. I still felt sick constantly, and it was on one of those nights that I got my next unpleasant surprise.

At the hotel in Anaheim, Kat and I were sharing a room, and Glenn, my tour manager, was next door. One night, as I lay next to Kat doing my best to manage my nausea, she suddenly said, "I'm just going to over to Glenn's room for a minute. I need to go through the accounts with him."

I nodded and didn't think any more of it until I woke an hour or so later. To begin with, I thought the sounds were coming from the TV, but when I turned it off I realized that the groans and half-stifled screams were coming from the room next door. I quickly glanced around and saw that I was alone in the room. With such a sinking feeling that it seemed to fill my entire body, I got up from the bed and stood with my ear to the wall.

I didn't have to listen for particularly long to realize that Glenn and Kat were having wild sex only a few feet away from me. Though our relationship had more or less fizzled out by that point, and though she could obviously sleep with whoever she wanted, in that moment it felt like a trapdoor had opened right beneath my feet.

I realized at once that it must have been going on for some time, maybe even since the start of the tour, and that Kat had made a conscious decision not to say anything to me. It felt like a real betrayal, and I lay down on the bed in some kind of shock. The fact that Glenn, who was married, was sleeping with Kat, who had a boyfriend back in England, didn't bother me at all—that was just what life on tour was like, and people could do whatever they wanted with their relationships, so long as it didn't affect their work. But I had always thought that Kat and I were honest with one another and that our relationship was also a friendship. That was what really hurt me.

Early the next morning, Kat came creeping back into the room. I pretended to wake up, though I had actually been lying awake all night.

"Everything OK with the accounts?" I asked in a natural-sounding tone.

"Yep," Kat said, her face innocent. "Glenn and I managed to go over loads of stuff relating to the merch. We've sold a lot of T-shirts, and the posters are doing well, too."

I ripped the phone from the socket in the wall and threw it at her across the room. She ducked at the last moment and stared back at me with a terror-stricken look. Then she started to sob.

That morning, after forcing down a couple of biscuits and a cup of tea, I phoned the Jive office in London and told them that Kat wasn't doing her job and that I was sending her home. Then I took Glenn to one side and fired him. I must have been radiating some kind of ice-cold fury, because his only attempts to defend himself were a couple of lame, weak remarks.

I had one gig left in Anaheim and then the tour was moving on to Canada, with shows scheduled for a number of huge, sold-out arenas. I was upset by Kat's betrayal and still very weak from the stomach bug, which was refusing to go away. On top of that, I no longer had a tour manager. So, with tears sticking in my throat, I called Mum and told her what had happened. I said, "I don't know how I'm going to cope."

Mum is the one person who has always been closest to me, and she instantly understood how serious things were. She said, "I'll bring Colin and we'll come over to be with you."

Colin was her new boyfriend, and they really did jump on the next plane to California, and flew from there to Canada.

Colin took on the role of tour manager, and with him and Mum at my side, I could relax a little and dare to believe that I might make it through the rest of the tour after all.

My welcome in Canada really was overwhelming. When the time came for my first show there, people were literally hanging from the streetlights in an attempt to catch a glimpse of me, and there were so many people knocking on the car windows and standing in the road that we only just made it into the festival area. It was a beautiful summer's evening, with a warm breeze, but as I went up on stage, I still felt cold.

In fact, I felt unwell throughout the entire show and couldn't really take in the incredible response from the crowd. When I eventually—after several encore songs—managed to leave the stage, I felt so bad that Mum reacted instinctively and rushed over to me. Just then, I vomited so violently that there was blood everywhere. I collapsed to the floor and Mum caught me in her arms, wiping the blood running down my chin with a tissue. She shouted for Colin to ring an ambulance.

Half an hour later, when we made it to the hospital, Mum held up the blood-soaked tissue to the doctor who came to meet us. It turned out that when my aunt Maureen had been seriously ill a few years earlier, the doctors had told Mum to save any blood she coughed up so that they could examine whether it was old or new. The Canadian doctor could see that the blood on the tissue was old, and immediately pushed a tube down my throat and pumped up a whole load of blood. After that, they pulled out the tube and started pushing a camera down the same way.

I was still awake and was completely panic stricken.

"No, no!" I shouted, grabbing the arm of the nurse closest to me. "What are you doing? I want to be put under!"

But clearly the situation was so serious that they didn't have time to do that. They managed to get the camera into my stomach, in any case, and everyone—Mum included—stared at the screens behind and above my head as though spellbound.

Mum later told me that it looked like a volcano was spouting blood into my stomach. Apparently the tablets I had taken to kill the parasite had been so strong that they corroded my stomach.

They kept me in under observation that night, and I had to lie in a room with a drip in my arm. Mum stayed by my side as I complained weakly, "How am I meant to sleep with this needle stuck in my arm?"

I felt completely awful, and the next day, when I realized I would have to cancel the upcoming show, everything felt even worse. As an artist, the last thing you want is to have to cancel a gig. I felt no better when I saw what a few of the papers were writing about me. Their headlines were screaming in huge, bold letters that I had ended up in hospital after taking an overdose.

It took me a few days to feel somewhat recovered. I had been given a medicine called Tagamet to restore the acidity levels in my stomach, and all I could do was wait for the wound to heal. During the month or so that was expected to take, the only things I was allowed to eat were easily digestible foods like white bread, boiled chicken, rice, soups, and bananas.

My life on the road started to resemble a health retreat for the elderly—with the one crucial difference that I was actually surrounded by party-hungry young men.

After seven shows in Canada, we crossed the border back into the US, where I played gigs in Chicago, New York, and Cleveland, among others, finally making it to the Six Flags Great Adventure park in New Jersey in July. By then, my support act was Cheap Trick, and Robin Zander and the other band members happened to be friends with Jon Bon Jovi's little brother, Matt Bongiovi, who turned up one day while we were doing our soundcheck.

"I know you hung out with my brother," Matt said, winking when we introduced ourselves.

Then he took the boys and me on a tour of the theme park. We tested plenty of the attractions, among them a completely crazy roller coaster that suddenly reminded me that my stomach wasn't quite back to normal yet.

Exactly a week later, I was booked to play a show at the famous Sands Casino Hotel in Atlantic City, still with Cheap Trick as my support act. During the sound check, I noticed that the area in front of the stage was full of tables, and I asked Colin to find out what was going on from the manager of the hotel. When he came back, he shouted, "He says there are a load of Russians coming to see you and that they wanted to eat while they're doing it."

"But Cheap Trick and I are rock acts," I shouted back, feeling my irritation grow. "We can't play for people who are sitting down having a meal. Tell the manager to come here."

When a stout, thin-haired man in a dark suit appeared in front of the stage, I told him exactly what I thought: that I wanted the audience to be standing while I performed. It was a rock concert, not dinnertime entertainment. Cabaret wasn't me.

"Oh, no, they've paid a lot of money," the manager said, raising his shoulders in an apologetic shrug that told me that he had no intention of compromising.

I had no choice but to bite the bullet, but that evening, when I saw those people sitting at their tables and talking away while we were playing, I was furious.

We did two more shows at the Sands, followed by a few more US gigs, before flying back to Canada for ten extra dates. I was so popular there that it seemed like I could fill as many arenas as I wanted. We began with a huge outdoor festival in Montreal and then worked our way right up to the island of Newfoundland.

I looked after my stomach with boring food, medicine, and disgusting health drinks. This time, the problem was with my voice. After the issues I'd had with my vocal cords in the past, losing my voice was practically my biggest fear.

I'd started working with a vocal coach in New York, one who had also helped people like Jon Bon Jovi and Cyndi Lauper. Her name was Katy Legrester, and so far on the tour, I had only needed to call her for help once. But suddenly, my throat was so hoarse that I panicked and threw myself at the phone.

"Katy!" I shouted down the line. "What should I do . . . can you hear how my voice sounds?"

"Easy, Sam, easy," Katy said, ordering me to do a couple of special vocal exercises and to drink a disgusting concoction—which, if I'm honest, I didn't bother with. Above all, she thought I should rest my voice as much as I could.

The hoarseness continued, and my throat felt like it was constricting even more at the thought of that evening's show to almost twenty thousand people in Ottawa. My backing singer Catherine had noticed how I was doing and told me to gargle an aspirin dissolved in water, swallowing a little at the very end.

"Believe me, it works," she said. I knew I could trust her, because she had worked in the industry for years with artists like David Bowie and Tina Turner.

So I gargled and swallowed, and the truth was that my voice felt a little better and held out for the entire show. I did the same ahead of the next show, with the same results. Because my stomach couldn't handle the acetylsalicylic acid, it did cause me some problems there, but that felt like a relatively small price to pay to not let down my fans.

18

RAFI CAMINO

Whenever we slept together, he wanted the room to be completely dark. And if we did it during the day, he would close all of the curtains so that you couldn't even see your hand in front of you. If I tried to turn on a lamp, he would rush to turn it off again.

"I think you need to move to Spain."

"What?!" I said, looking up in surprise from the papers Dad had asked me to sign in his little office in Crouch End.

"Yeah, otherwise you'll end up paying out all the money in tax."

We had just been talking about the new contract that had arrived from my record label. According to Dad, they were offering a million pounds for five records. The old contract was about to expire, and they seemed very keen to renew it.

"So I can't live here at all?" I asked.

"Of course you can, but only for a certain number of days a year. You have to spend the rest of the time abroad, so Spain seems like a good option."

It wasn't that I had anything against Spain. I'd been there plenty of times, both on holiday and with work, and I really did appreciate the warmth, the sunshine, and the food. But I also loved my England and had trouble seeing how I would cope with living away from family and friends for so long. It was true that I had been on the road a lot and that I had lived in New York for some time, but this felt more like a definitive exile.

"I don't know . . ." I began.

"Trust me, Sam," said Dad. "It's the only way."

And so I believed him. How could I have known that he hadn't read the new contract from Jive properly? If he had, he would have seen that I had to sell at least a million copies of each record to see any of that money. But that was something my lawyers would discover only much later.

With a sense that I soon wouldn't really have anywhere to call home, I flew to New York the next day. From there, I went on to Los Angeles, where I had been invited to take part in a sitcom called *Charles in Charge*. The show was in its fifth and final season, starring the actor Scott Baio. He'd been a teenage star in the legendary American TV show *Happy Days*, but he had since grown up and become a director, too. The plan was for him to both direct and star in this particular episode, in which I would play a British pop star called Samantha Steele. She came from Sheffield, the Steel City, so the surname was a terrible pun.

Scott Baio had specifically requested that the producer book me to act opposite him, and the scriptwriters had created the role especially for me. I assumed Scott just wanted to use me because I was so big in the US right then.

"So that's what you think?" my former bodyguard Dave said with a smile as he picked me up from the airport and drove me back to his apartment late that night.

Dave had moved to Hollywood to try his luck as a stuntman, and he was letting me stay with him while the filming was underway.

"Yeah?" I said, not understanding what he meant. It later turned out Scott was a huge fan.

The next day, at the studio, I struck up a conversation with John Travolta's sister, Ellen, who played Scott's mother in the show. I liked her, because she reminded me of so many of the women I had grown up with. Later on, she would come over to me several times and say, with a wink, "John would love you."

I didn't say anything; I just smiled with embarrassment and thought, *Oh, my God!* John Travolta had left an indelible mark on me as a twelve- or thirteen-year-old, when I saw him in *Saturday Night Fever* and *Grease*.

In any case, my character, Samantha Steele, would happen to be photographed alongside Charles, i.e., Scott, and when the pictures appeared in a gossip magazine, there would be a whole load of misunderstanding.

In one of the scenes, Scott and I had to kiss, so he started winding me up, saying, "I bet you're a bad kisser, so we had better practice." I've always loved kissing, so I didn't mind.

He kissed me deeply, for a long time, in front of all the camera men, actors, scriptwriters, lighting technicians, makeup artists, and everyone else in the studio. I almost lost my breath several times. But in the end, he seemed happy, and we could go for the first take.

"Cut!" Scott suddenly shouted. "We need to practice one more time."

And then he kissed me again, for so long that it started to feel embarrassing. We eventually managed to finish not only that scene but all of the other takes I would appear in. Scott praised me for my part and, in his very next breath, invited me to visit his place the next day.

I went to visit him, and we kissed again. We made out. The thought of having sex felt like it was much too soon. I asked whether he wanted to do something the next day.

"That would've been great," he said. "But I'm busy watching the Super Bowl with my dad." When I told Dave where I had been, he just smiled. Late the next evening, when he got back to his apartment after going on a small club crawl, he said, almost in passing, "I saw Scott."

"Where?" I asked, not taking my eyes from the TV.

"In a club—with a load of birds."

I looked over to him then, and he sighed gently and shrugged. "He's a player, Sam."

Scott called me the next day, but I didn't bother to answer. I had already erased him from my memory, and he soon seemed to do the same. Not long after that, he was in a relationship with Pamela Anderson.

Before I left LA, there was one important thing I needed to tick off—a meeting with Clive Calder, the head of Jive Records, to discuss my future with the label. Clive had invited me over for dinner, so I pulled on a nice dress and took a taxi to his place.

His house really did testify to his success, and it impressed me— even if I didn't show it as he welcomed me in.

We sat down at the table almost immediately, and started to talk as we ate.

"I've been thinking a little," Clive said, taking a sip of what was probably a very expensive wine. "And I have a few ideas."

He was the boss, after all, and it was his home, so I let him continue without saying anything.

"Wait, let me play something so you understand what I mean." He got up from the table and went over to the stereo at the other end of the room. As though he had picked it out in advance, he quickly grabbed a record and put it on. Music began streaming from the extremely elegant speakers, and before I had time to guess what it was, he shouted, "Paula Abdul. Something like this would be perfect for you."

At first, I thought he was pulling my leg, but when I realized he wasn't, I said, "Sorry, Clive, but this isn't at all what I want to do. I like dance beats, but there has to be a guitar riff in them."

He came back to the table and sat down with a concerned frown. It was as though he couldn't work out why I didn't understand this thing he thought was obvious. "So what type of music do you want to make? Give me an example of an artist you like."

I racked my brains and threw out a name: "Roxette. They play the kind of edgy rock pop I want to make. Have you heard them?"

He hadn't, despite the fact that "The Look" had been number one in the charts only six months earlier, and that they'd had several big US hits since.

"Listen to me now, Sam," Clive said in a tone that revealed he was used to getting his own way. "Your voice doesn't work for rock, and you'll never make it as a rock singer. You're no Lita Ford."

"How do you know that?" I asked, feeling the anger rising. "At my shows, I cover KISS, Joan Jett, and Pat Benatar. That's more my style than this." I nodded in the direction of the record player. "But you clearly wouldn't know, because you've never once come to see me, despite the fact I've toured the entire US."

The creases on Clive's forehead grew deeper, but it was as though he had made up his mind to ignore all of my arguments. He went back over to the stereo and changed the record.

"Bobby Brown," he shouted over the mic. "We'll bet on the black market, because you're the only white girl who's topped the black charts."

"But I want guitars," I shouted back.

I don't know how many times I'd had to say it—often in an incredibly irritated tone—to producers, songwriters, studio engineers, and others. Sometimes, it felt like none of them were interested in finding out who I was from a musical perspective, or what suited me best. In the studio, I could usually get my own way—in some critical cases by threatening not to record the track—but with Clive, that wouldn't work. His will was as strong as mine, and when I left his house that evening, we had only really agreed on one thing: that we had completely different opinions on which way my career should go.

The very next day, I heard Dad's voice screaming down the phone: "What have you done?!" Though he answered the question himself: "You've just fucked it for yourself! Clive doesn't want to renew your contract."

I said that I had just been honest when Clive played me music I didn't like. I simply couldn't see myself recording, promoting, making videos for, and performing material I didn't believe in.

Dad sounded like he was about to explode across the Atlantic in England, but I didn't care what he said, especially not since I could hear that he was drunk again. Just a few years later, he would derail a huge record deal himself, simply because he couldn't bear the thought of letting anyone else take care of my management in the US.

But as I sat there with him shouting down the line, I was more irritated at the fact that not even he understood what it was I wanted to do. If it was up to him, I would have still been going around doing PAs and singing playback.

I did, at least, follow his advice and move to Spain. In fact, I barely had time to leave LA before he had found me a nice flat in an apartment complex in the small port town of Puerto Banús, not far from Marbella. Quite a few other celebrities had apartments and houses there, too, people like Sean Connery, Julio Iglesias, and Rod Stewart. There were also a couple of shadier celebrities living in my area, people I quickly got to know and spend time with. They were Freddie Foreman and Ronnie Knight, the English gangsters, both part of the "famous five"—five equally famous and notorious English criminals who were wanted by the English police and lived in Spain. Back then, there was no extradition treaty between Spain and England, which is why the English press often referred to the Costa del Sol as the Costa del Crime.

Freddie and Ronnie were primarily famous for allegedly carrying out the so-called "Security Express" robbery, which, at the time, was the biggest in UK history. They were both from the East End, which is possibly why we got on so well. But I also had plenty of other friends and acquaintances there, among them the singer Mel Williams, whom I also recorded a song with. And on the road up to Ronda, not far from Marbella, Glenn Tipton, the guitarist from Judas Priest, had a house that was still being built. He lived there all the same, and had a huge recording studio with fantastic views out towards Africa through its enormous panoramic windows. It was in that very studio that, among other things, he recorded a great guitar solo for my track "Spirit of America."

Living in Spain as a Brit, you quickly develop a sense of being on some kind of never-ending holiday. Everything is comfortable, not least the climate, and you turn to habits that might not be so healthy in the long run. At least, that's how it was for me. Simply put, I partied quite a lot after I got settled into my new flat. A whole gang of us went up into the mountains by the town of Álora, for example, had a barbecue, and slept beneath the stars. We drank and smoked, and quite a few lines were done. Cocaine was something I hadn't tried before, but since I'd seen my dad do lines regularly over the past few years, it was like it had been normalized for me. Dad was also the person who offered me my very first line.

He had always been introverted and quiet, the type of man who, at parties, would sit on his own in a corner, watching people while he methodically got himself drunk. He never danced, never joked, never showed any feelings or the slightest indication that he was having a good time. But when he came to visit me in Spain, he did a lot of coke during a party in the flat in Marbella, and it was as though he had suddenly gained the self-confidence he had been lacking all his life.

I just stared at him, I could barely believe my eyes. He was dancing as though he was a natural, and was charming everyone around him. I almost wished Mum could have been there to see him. I mean, she loved to dance and had spent so many years trying in vain to tempt him onto various dance floors. So, when he asked whether I wanted any, the answer was obvious.

The thing with drugs is that they affect different people in different ways. For someone like Dad, cocaine was as wonderful as it was dangerous. It gave him confidence and took his reserved self away. The odd joint to relax was more my thing, so it never got hold on me—I could take it or leave it. It also didn't take me long to see the impact of the drugs, not just on Dad but on many of the other people around me. They became cokeheads far more quickly than they expected, and things went quickly down hill from there.

I tried to talk about it with Dad on several occasions, but by then he was already on the way to ruin and didn't want to listen. It annoyed me, especially because I sometimes felt that he was acting like a teenager. This was a man who had always been in control of everything and who I had, in many ways, respected, but he started being careless with bookings and things like that, and I found myself having to deal with problems that were actually his responsibility more and more often.

A few days later, for example, I was due to take part in a live broadcast of a Spanish TV show, and I had to go alone. It was a really posh production where the audience sat at tables in tuxedos and ballgowns, watching the performers on stage. Something about it provoked me—or maybe bored me would be more accurate—and when my turn came round, I jumped up onto one of the long tables and walked from one end to the other while I sang. It was a bit like in the film *Hair*, and just like in the film, the people sitting at the table looked terrified and tried to rescue their glasses while they also flinched back—all apart from one man, who looked more amused.

He was a handsome young man with jet-black, back-combed hair and sharp features, and as I stood in front of him, he took a rose from the table decoration and handed it to me. I took the rose as I continued to sing, and I kept glancing in his direction.

Once the show was over and I had gone to my dressing room to catch my breath, there was a sudden knock at the door. I opened it and was met with a polite smile from a short, slightly grey-haired man who, in heavily accented but perfectly correct English, told me that there was someone who wanted to see me.

"Aha?" I said, sounding bored. "Who's that?"

"The one who gave you the rose," the man replied. "He really wants to say hello."

"Ah, him! Tell him I'd be happy to see him."

When he came to my dressing room, I was blinded by his smile and handsome face and felt an instant connection. We arranged to go out the following evening.

His name was Rafael Comino, but he went by Rafi. When I asked him what he did, I initially didn't understand his answer, because he spoke English so badly (which was probably why he had gotten one of his friends to ask me out).

"You're a butcher?!" I said, sounding surprised, as he mimed a cow or bull with his fingers as horns, and then kind of stabbed the air with an invisible knife.

The limo driver explained that Rafi was one of Spain's best bullfighters and came from the finest bullfighting family in the country. His father was a living legend and regarded almost as royalty by many Spaniards.

But how could I have known that? I had just moved to Spain and wasn't the least bit interested in bullfighting. What little of it I'd seen on TV only filled me with disgust.

Though obviously I didn't say any of that to Rafi during our dinner at one of Madrid's better restaurants, because he wasn't just handsome, he was a real gentleman. So, instead, I did what I could to seem interested in his job, and maybe I did a little too well— suddenly, he invited me to his next bullfight in Seville a few days later. Or, more accurately, Rafi's interpreter (who sat with us for the entire meal) did.

"Uh, thanks," I said with a strained smile.

Rafi's grin grew wider and he whispered a few words in Spanish to the interpreter, who turned to me and said, "Good, I'll send a private plane . . . to pick you up . . ."

What Rafi probably hadn't counted on was that my Mum, Celeste, and Natalie (whom I had met in New York) were in Marbella at the time, along with several other friends. Nor that I would be bringing them all with me on the plane. But if he was disappointed that he didn't get me all to himself, he hid it well, and we were given great seats in the bullfighting arena in Seville. Sadly, that meant we also got slightly too clear a view of what was actually happening in the ring. You could hear every little sound and smell the blood in the close, still air. To be honest, I found the whole thing repulsive, and if I'd had even the slightest of opportunities, I would have run a mile. But, instead, I was forced to vomit into an empty cigarette packet and then try to look completely indifferent. All the same, when a couple of Spanish journalists outside the arena asked what I thought of my debut bullfighting experience, I couldn't help but tell them the truth: "I hated every second of it."

Not that it stopped me from continuing to see Rafi, and he didn't seem particularly upset that I didn't want to go to any more fights. Instead, he took me to his childhood home in Madrid.

I don't know quite what I had expected, but it wasn't the huge palace we pulled up at on the outskirts of the Spanish capital. Rafi moved through that environment with the same degree of ease as I felt lost. His parents weren't home, and I got the feeling that they were deliberately staying away to avoid meeting me. I suppose I wasn't exactly the match they had been hoping for their son. His interpreter was there, however, translating as best as he could whenever Rafi told stories about growing up in the palace.

But it was actually only after the interpreter had left that I got my first glimpse of the real Rafi, who turned out to be extremely shy. Whenever we slept together, he wanted the room to be completely dark. And if we did it during the day, he would close all of the curtains so that you couldn't even see your hand in front of you. If I tried to turn on a lamp, he would rush to turn it off again. It felt a little strange, and things got even stranger when I realized that Rafi had lied to me about his age. He had told me we were the same age, but in actual fact he was three years younger—something I naturally didn't care about.

Whenever we were out and about, female admirers would come up to him, and I quickly realized just how famous he was in Spain. But rather than feeling jealous, I was almost proud that he was so coveted. Rafi, on the other hand, hated all of the attention, publicity, and paparazzi. And yes, I can understand that; we could barely leave my apartment in Marbella without being surrounded on the street, and we would be followed by streams of cars and motorbikes driving at breakneck speed whenever we tried to go anywhere.

Sometimes, Rafi would swear loudly in Spanish. If we went to the beach, he would set up a ring of open parasols to protect us from any onlookers. Our only unobstructed view was out towards the sea. But he still never relaxed, and if he saw a boat glittering out at sea, he would grab my arm, point, and say, "Paparazzi!"

He was probably right that it was the sun reflecting off a camera lens. Rafi knew all the tricks the paparazzi used, and he quickly opened more parasols and placed them in front of us. With that, we could no longer see the sea, either.

As a result, we barely left my apartment whenever he came to visit, and since I spoke no Spanish and he knew hardly any English, that meant long silences whenever the interpreter wasn't there. All Rafi could really say in English was, "You are the most beautiful girl in the world for me." And though that was obviously nice to hear, it got a bit repetitive in the long run. Especially once I moved back to England and we tried to keep our relationship alive over the phone. The silences and the declarations of love became very trying for me. I think Rafi must have heard it in my voice, because he soon bought himself a Spanish-English/English-Spanish dictionary and would sit with it in front of him whenever we spoke. Sadly, that didn't make things any better. Now, instead of silence, I would hear him leafing frantically through the book, searching for the right words. It would take him an eternity to come up with even one sentence, and if I then said anything in reply, he would shout, "One minute, one minute, I have to look in the book!"

I groaned quietly and felt like strangling myself with the phone cord.

My telephone bills became astronomical, and obviously the relationship wasn't sustainable in the long run. So, one day, I told him it was over. Hand on heart, I have to admit that I was never really in love with Rafi. It was more that he was so handsome, I couldn't stop myself.

19

SOUTH AMERICA

They took the partying to new levels, despite
me trying to hold them back. Even my bodyguard,
Chris, got drawn into it, as did Will, who went
more or less bananas from all the cocaine and booze.

I felt like the Beatles as I cast an anxious glance at the chaos surrounding us in the arrivals hall at El Dorado International Airport. People were screaming and grabbing at me, asking for my autograph as the camera flashes blinded me and journalists from newspapers and TV channels stuck microphones in my face. A moment later, as I was pushed out to the limousine that would take me, Dad, Paula, my bodyguard Chris, and my tour manager, Will, to our hotel, it really was like running the gauntlet. There were horns blaring and people climbing fences, sitting in trees, and standing on car roofs to catch a glimpse of me. It was like some out-of-control carnival as I walked towards the car with Chris, who was doing everything he could to stop me from being crushed.

"Get in the car, Sam!"he hissed out of the corner of his mouth. "Get in the bloody car!"

Bogotá was one of the last stops in a long line of South American shows, which were unlike anything I had ever experienced before. I mean, as we drove from the airport, we had a whole group of police motorbikes in front of us, their sirens blaring, and a long line of cars behind. The chaos continued on the motorway. People were hanging out of car windows and holding up huge posters of my face; some were even standing on the roofs of the cars driving alongside us.

"They're completely insane," Paula decided.

"There haven't been any foreign acts here since Earth, Wind & Fire, and that was years ago," said Will.

"You can tell," I said, staring out of the window at a man blowing me kisses with both hands rather than holding the wheel.

The road outside the hotel was packed with people, too, and when Paula and I finally made it up to our suite on the top floor, we just looked at one another and burst out laughing. The entire situation was absurd, terrifying almost.

I went out onto the balcony and cautiously looked down at the street, which was full of people as far as the eye could see. There must have been thousands of them, and the minute they spotted me, they started screaming.

"I have to give them something," I said to Paula, digging out a couple of T-shirts from one of my suitcases. I went back out to the balcony.

Paula followed me and watched as I let one T-shirt after another sail down to the street below. People had their arms up in the air, and before any of the T-shirts even landed, full-blown fights had broken out all around them.

"For God's sake, Sam, remember we're in Colombia," said Paula. "You keep that up, they'll start shooting each other soon."

That evening, we played a huge arena, Coliseo el Campín, and we left for Medellín the very next day. We held a press conference while we were still at the airport, because we wanted the papers, radio, and TV to know that it really was me—and not some lookalike—who had arrived in town, and that I had my entire band with me. We'd heard that people in that part of the world were used to being duped, so we wanted to let them know that on my tour, they'd get what they paid for.

As I sat in my dressing room later that evening, catching my breath after yet another gig with an utterly fantastic crowd, a man came backstage to talk to me. I immediately realized that he must have some kind of status, because not just anyone could get past the rigorous security arrangements. He took my hand and said a few kind words about the show before getting straight to the point:

"What are you doing tomorrow evening?"

"Not much," I replied. "We have a day off and we're leaving for the next gig the day after that."

"If I give you fifty thousand, do you think you could do a forty- or fifty-minute set? My daughter turns twenty-one tomorrow, and I'd like to surprise her."

I stared at him. He was in his fifties and was very well dressed, but there was something tense about his mouth. I assumed he must be a rich businessman of some kind.

In any case, fifty thousand dollars in extra income was great, particularly if you had a load of musicians, dancers, and other staff to take care of like I did. So, I said, "Sure, let's do it!"

The man smiled and immediately took an enormous wad of notes from the inner pocket of his pale, tailored jacket. He counted out the aforementioned amount.

"Payment in advance, so I can be sure you'll come."

He handed me the money with a smile that had vanished before he even turned to leave.

Maybe I should have realized what kind of guy he was right there and then. Regardless, a little light came on in my head when the boys from the band and I arrived at his house a short distance outside of Medellín. We were picked up by two SUVs outside the hotel, and they drove us up into the mountains. When I saw all the guards with automatic weapons and bulletproof vests guarding the mansion-like villa and its magnificent gardens, both behind secure white walls, I whispered to Will, "Something tells me this bloke doesn't make his money growing oranges."

But rather than looking concerned, Will just smiled at what I had awkwardly tried to suggest. It wasn't until after we'd played to the birthday girl in a room that looked more like a ballroom than a lounge that I saw him put two and two together.

In any case, the man took us riding in the mountains the next day. The boys and I could barely sit upright on the horses, since we'd been up partying all night, and Will was practically slumped forward on his horse.

"Will!" I whispered, my eyes sweeping across the bodyguards riding all around us. Each one seemed to be armed with an automatic weapon. "Listen! Maybe he's just got loads of money and is worried about being kidnapped."

But Will didn't reply. He just gave a hoarse laugh before straightening up with a groan.

I do have to say that Colombia was a lot of fun. The boys certainly seemed to like it, anyway, but for very different reasons. They took the partying to new levels, despite me trying to hold them back. Even my bodyguard, Chris, got drawn into it, as did Will, who went more or less bananas from all the cocaine and booze.

The next stop on the tour was Barranquilla, on the Atlantic coast. Since we arrived in the middle of the night, I decided that we would hold our usual press conference at nine the next morning. That way, news of the concert that evening would have time to reach people during the day.

"So I can rely on you being here to sort everything out for nine?" I asked Will as we stood in the lobby of the beach hotel.

Will gave me the thumbs-up and then disappeared off to the bar.

My guitarist, Lol Ford, and several other members of the band joined him. I went up to my room, but I had trouble sleeping because I was so worried about not waking up in time.

By eight the next morning, I was sick of twisting and turning in bed, so I went over to the window to check that everything had been set up down by the pool where the press conference would take place. But I couldn't see a table or any chairs, and there was no sign of any posters or other PR material. I immediately dialed the number for Will's room, and when he didn't pick up, I ran out into the corridor and knocked on Paula's door.

"We need to find Will," I said when she answered.

We ran around the hotel together, but there was no sign of him, and so we made our way down to the beach. There, on his back at the water's edge, still wearing his white linen suit, was Will. He was unconscious, and the water was already up to his knees. If we hadn't found him right then, he probably would have drowned.

"Will!" I shouted, but there was no reaction. I bent down and gave him a hard slap, which did at least make him force one eye open. Paula and I each took one arm and we helped him to his feet. I noticed that the water had made his trouser legs shrink, which really didn't look good, but it was the only suit he had, and he had no choice but to meet the press in a pair of trousers that were far too short for him. Sadly, he was so far gone that he couldn't even answer any of their questions. I managed to hide my anger, but I also decided, right there and then, that I was going to fire him.

I should have done it as soon as we got to Bolivia, because when we arrived, we realized that, in his drug-fueled haze, Will had been wrong about the date—meaning we had missed our first show in La Paz. The promoter was furious, of course, demanding money from us because he had been forced to issue refunds for tickets. That led to a number of meetings between him and Will, while the band and I were scheduled to play another show just outside of town.

The only problem was that when we got to the arena for sound check, all of our equipment had been seized. The police quickly turned up and took us back to the hotel, where they told us we were being held under house arrest until the promoter had been paid.

There was a hint of *The Shining* about the whole thing—not just because we were the only guests in the hotel, but also because it felt like virtually anything could happen. And, in a sense, it did.

That evening, when we went down to the dining room to eat a simple dinner, all of the lights suddenly went out. Since we were already worried about the situation, it really didn't feel good. I mean, within the course of a few seconds, the room was pitched into complete darkness, and we suddenly heard thudding, knocking, and shouting coming from somewhere outside.

"Quick, get under the table!" someone yelled.

I threw myself to the floor and quickly made my way beneath the long table. The blood was pounding in my temples, and I had the feeling that something horrible was about to happen. It hardly got any better when I heard Paula sob, "They're going to kill us."

Next thing I knew, the door to the dining room flew open with a bang and the lights came back on. I peered out from beneath the table and saw the legs of a group of men striding towards us.

"Come out!" one of them shouted, and as we stood in front of them a moment later, I prepared myself for the worst.

A man with a huge, black moustache pointed to me and said, "You will have to come with us. We will take you somewhere and wait for ransom."

But Will suddenly plucked up some courage and moved between me and the man.

"No one is leaving before I've made a phone call."

And then he left to make that call—to the American embassy, as it turned out. Less than half an hour later, two bureaucrats from the embassy turned up and, without further discussion, took me away with them. They took me to the embassy, where I was able to stay under their protection, while the band and the others remained at the hotel, refusing to leave the country while I was still there. They just wanted to make sure that nothing had happened to me, and after I had spent five days under house arrest in the embassy, Dad arrived in La Paz with a briefcase full of money. Once we paid the promoter the sum he claimed we owed him, our equipment was finally returned to us, and we were able to continue the tour.

20

INDIA

Completely without warning, and as though on command, every single man lifted up his longshirt—which I've heard are known as kurtas—and I found myself staring at more penises than I'd ever seen in my life.

In my part of London, there was a tobacconist that I went to practically every day when I was home, to buy newspapers or cigarettes. He came from India and still had a large number of family members there. We used to make small talk with one another, and one day, out of sheer curiosity, I asked whether he thought anyone in India knew who I was.

"Oh yes!" he said. "You're very big in India! Very big."

"What?" I said, genuinely surprised. "Are you serious?"

"Oh, yes!" he repeated with a smile. "Everybody knows you there."

Later that day, I went over to Dad's house and told him what the tobacconist had said. Dad seemed at least as surprised as I was, but he managed to get in touch with a promoter over there. The man, Venkat Vardhan, confirmed what the tobacconist had said: I *had*, despite being completely oblivious to it, a huge following in India. Not long after that, I was booked to play gigs in New Delhi, Mumbai, Calcutta, and Madras.

Since we were pretty tight musically at that point in time, I took the same band to India that I'd had with me in South America.

We had an entire Air India plane to ourselves on the flight out, and when we landed in Delhi I barely had time to disembark before someone had hung a string of flowers around my neck and given me a red dot on my forehead. After that, it was just a case of walking the red carpet that had been laid out on the ground by the plane, with people bowing to my left and my right. I didn't feel entirely comfortable with the situation, as I was still a very working-class girl and felt embarrassed. And things got even stranger when we went to leave the airport and I saw that people had strung huge banners across the road reading, "Welcome to India, Princess Samantha!"

We could barely move for the crowds, and I seriously wondered whether they might have mistaken me for some member of the royal family. I had the same feeling that something must have gone wrong when the promoter drove us to the arena ahead of the first gig. It was an enormous sports stadium named after India's first prime minister, Jawaharlal Nehru, and which, according to the promoter, held seventy thousand people. We had been told that we might be playing to audiences of maybe five thousand people, so I just stared at the promoter when he explained with a smile that all three nights had sold out.

"It's bigger than the crowd record set by Bruce Springsteen when he was here a few years ago."

The promoter was beaming with pride, but I was more concerned. I mean, we didn't have nearly enough lights or a big enough PA for such a large show.

Not long later, we held a crisis meeting at the hotel, and after twisting and turning the dilemma, someone remembered that Jethro Tull were currently also on tour in India. One phone call later, the problem was solved. We could borrow their equipment, meaning that the following evening, on schedule, we played the first of what would be ten sold-out shows.

Lots of things were different in that country. Not just the fact that the audiences were huge, but also that they consisted almost exclusively of men. Or at least that's what I thought when I first ran out on stage and studied the crowd. But then I spotted the women in the stands, dancing in their long saris. Sadly, they weren't allowed to dance among the men, who had a completely different way of showing their appreciation.

It started out innocently, when they began throwing what I thought were rolls of toilet paper at the stage. At least, they looked like toilet paper rolls, unfurling in mid-air and landing at my feet, but when I took a closer look I realized they were turbans. And so I waved happily at them.

Then, completely without warning, and as though on command, every single man lifted up his longshirt—which I've heard are known as kurtas—and I found myself staring at more penises than I'd ever seen in my life. The whole thing was completely absurd, and it didn't get any better when the men all started shouting, "Samantha! Samantha!" in unison, smiling happily as they did it.

I was so shocked that I completely forgot the words to the song I was singing. I mean, focusing on the lyrics isn't so easy when you have several thousand men doing the propeller in front of you, seemingly thinking it's completely normal. The men did the same thing at least once during every song, and when I went backstage to take a breather during the break before the encore, I said to my assistant, Paula, "You won't believe this, but pretty much every geezer in the crowd has been flashing his dick at me!"

For understandable reasons, Paula didn't look like she believed me, but as soon as I went back out on stage, she rushed up to the side of the stage. And when I glanced over to her from time to time, I saw her alternating between being completely appalled and laughing uncontrollably. She stood at the side of the stage during the next show, too, watching the men who, again, couldn't help but expose themselves to me.

By that point, I wasn't paying so much attention to it, because the band and I had developed Delhi belly, and we were doing everything we could to avoid shitting ourselves. We'd placed a line of buckets behind the stage, and between songs one or more of us would rush back there to empty our bowels. Towards the end of the show, I even had to do it in the middle of a song, and I ran over to the drummer and shouted (just like I had at Disneyland, when I'd had a parasite in my stomach), "Do a drum solo!"

Still, I wasn't the worst. My guitarist, Lol Ford, was so ill that he didn't even have time to run—he literally shat himself right there on stage. Ordinarily, I would go over to him during his guitar solo, but there was no way I could do it then; he smelled so bad.

He was just as ill the next day, and someone came up with the idea of putting bicycle clips at the bottom of his trousers, so at least the shit wouldn't run out onto the stage floor.

I have to say that Lol was brave when that happened, but I was furious with him a couple of days later, when we were due to play in Mumbai. As usual before the show, I'd had a meet and greet with the sponsors and other people whose hands I had to shake. That kind of thing was always a pain in the arse, because I needed to rest my voice. As a singer, you aren't really even meant to talk before going on stage, you're just meant to warm up your voice using various exercises, but I had no choice but to mingle and talk to these people who had paid for the whole package. It meant I wasn't in a particularly good mood when I left my dressing room that evening, and things didn't get any better as I was about to walk on stage.

We always used to start the show by playing the theme from *2001: A Space Odyssey*, *Also sprach Zarathustra* by Richard Strauss. It was the same music that Elvis had used to open his Las Vegas shows.

So, while the music from the film thundered out across the arena, my musicians got into position. I was at the side of the stage, waiting to make my entrance, when I noticed that Lol was missing. Since he was my lead guitarist, we couldn't start the show without him, and I felt my pulse pick up. Where the hell was he?

Back during the South America tour, Lol had already driven me mad on a number of occasions. It wasn't that he didn't do his job. The problem was that he never played the same from one day to the next; he was always adding or taking something away from the songs. Every night was different, and it meant I would be left standing there, waiting for a solo or something else that never came, all because he had suddenly decided that he didn't feel like playing it. That, in turn, knocked my confidence, and I would start thinking, *Am I the one missing something here?*

Now he wasn't even in position. I saw John, Paul, and the others looking at one another, and could practically feel the fear digging its claws into them. In less than one minute, the first song was meant to begin.

Right then, I saw Lol slouching towards me backstage, his guitar in one hand and a huge plastic bag in the other.

"Where the hell have you been?" I shouted, gesturing for him to go straight out and join the others.

Lol was so out of breath that he couldn't manage a single word, but he did have a stupid—and, in my eyes, provocative—smile on his sweaty face when he dropped the bag.

I cast a quick glance into it and saw that it was full of weed. The idiot had been off scoring drugs and probably got caught in traffic on the way back to the arena. He had put the entire gig at risk for a bit of weed.

I had to force myself not to look at him during the show, because I had an almost uncontrollable urge to strangle him. He was an old friend, but I fired him not long after that.

21

THE BETRAYAL

If you can't trust your own father, who can you trust?

Looking back, I've asked myself over and over again whether I shouldn't have realized what was going on. But the problem was, it all took place behind my back, and the person who betrayed me was also the one I trusted most in the world. I mean, if you can't trust your own father, who can you trust?

The prelude to what would become the darkest point of my life took place in autumn 1991. Dad and I had been to Norway on business, meeting a company that wanted my endorsement to launch a line of leather clothing. The flight home was relatively short, but Dad still managed to get completely wasted in the time between our arrival at the airport in Oslo and landing in London. By that point, his drink and drug abuse was completely out of control, and I had been forced to virtually become my own manager when it came to bookings, meetings, and other things. It felt uncertain, difficult, lonely, and incredibly frustrating. Especially considering he was still in charge of all of my money. It was only recently—as a twenty-five-year-old—that I had been allowed to get my own credit card. Before that, I'd had to ask Dad for pocket money, even when I lived in New York. He always wanted to know why I needed it, and it was the same even after I got the credit card. Every month, he would go through the statement to see what I had bought.

Another example of his controlling behavior was our living arrangement. Dad had bought two houses next door to one another in North London. They were both in his name, since I officially— and for the most part actually—lived in Spain. He moved into one of the houses, and I would stay in the other whenever I came back home with work or to visit. I had sold the house in Hertfordshire in conjunction with my move to Spain.

When our taxi pulled up that cool autumn evening, I followed Dad into his house. I wanted to make sure he got in OK, considering his drunken state. I held the door open for him so that he could take a couple of unsteady steps over the threshold with a half-empty bottle of duty-free vodka in one hand.

"Thanks, princess," he said, smirking almost mockingly and flashing the hole where he'd had a front tooth knocked out as a young hotel bell boy—he had gone into the lunch room at Claridges and jokingly waved a dummy pistol in the air.

It hurt me slightly, because he had always called me "princess" in a loving way when I was younger.

I'd dragged his bag inside from the taxi, and I put it down in the hallway and went over to the phone. I wanted to call Dave, who was temporarily back from LA, before it got too late, to ask whether he'd had time to install the new car stereo I'd bought while I was away. Dad was actually the one who was meant to be doing it, but over a month had passed without any sign of him helping me like he'd promised, and so I had asked Dave to do it instead.

"Hi Dave," I said into the receiver, "I just wanted to check whether you'd managed to fit the stereo."

I barely had time to say the words before I caught a movement out of the corner of one eye. I turned and saw Dad charging towards me with a mad look on his face. He ripped the phone from my hand and hit me. My field of vision went dark, and I staggered backwards as a single thought flashed through my mind: *I have to try to protect my face.*

"It's me who should be doing it, not that bastard," I heard Dad roar as I dizzily retreated into a corner of the hallway.

I had known for some time that Dad hated Dave. It was because Dave saw right through him and did everything he could to protect me, but it still came as a real shock that he could take that hate out on me like this. His attack also made me furious, and so I shouted, "You touch me again and I swear you'll regret it for the rest of your life, you fucking drunk."

I didn't have time to raise my hands before he hit my face. I fell to the floor and tried to curl up as tight as I could, because I knew it wasn't over yet. Dad started kicking me as he shouted, "You look like your fucking mother! You're just like her!"

I felt something break in my chest, followed by an indescribable pain and two thoughts filling my mind: *He's going to kill you. You need to get away.*

I tried to get up, but he kicked me so hard in the stomach that I was completely winded.

"Please, Dad, stop it," I managed, but it was like I couldn't get through to him.

I think it was probably sheer survival instinct that made me start to crawl towards the door as the kicks and blows continued to rain down on me. I eventually made it out onto the pavement. Dad paused in the doorway, threw the bottle at me, and shouted: "I'm the one who's meant to sort out the stereo—not him! You hear me?!"

I half crawled, half staggered across the road and knocked on the door of a neighbor called Nelly Bartlett. She stared at me with a horrified expression when she opened the door.

"Jesus Christ, what's happened?"

I told her the truth—that Dad had beaten me up.

"Can you call the police for me?"

But instead of doing as I asked, she said, "Really think about it, Sam, think about it. I'm sure Pat didn't mean it. He loves you—I know that. You'll ruin his life if you report him."

I couldn't believe my ears. Here I was, standing in front of her a battered mess, and all she could think about was protecting Dad.

She took me in and called Dave.

"Hi, I was just about to come over to your place," he said in an extremely concerned tone. "It sounded so strange when I got cut off. Has something happened?"

I asked him to come over as quickly as he could and said that I would explain everything when I saw him.

When Dave arrived a while later, he worked out what had happened without me needing to say a word. With a dogged look on his face, he said, "I'm going to kill that bastard."

I hurried to grab his arm.

"No, we're just going to leave right now. I don't want to stay here a second longer."

Dave took a deep breath and nodded. Then he helped me out to his car.

"Sam, you might have broken something. We should really take you to hospital to get it checked out."

"You know what'll happen then," I said, meaning it would be splashed across the front pages the next day.

Dave knew I was right, and he shook his head with a muffled growl and started the engine. He drove me over to Mum's house, followed me inside, and tried to calm her down as he cleaned and bandaged my wounds. There was a deep gash on my forehead, I had a black eye, and my body was covered in bruises. My hair was matted with blood from a wound on the back of my head, and I had a terrible pain in my chest.

I barely slept a wink that night. Early the next morning, Dave and I drove over to Dad's house again, and I stayed in the car while Dave walked down the garden path and rang the bell. A moment later, I saw Dad peering out of one of the windows, but he didn't open the door. Dave shouted, "Come out, Pat. Come and do what you did to Sam to me!"

Then he looked up at Dad, who was still standing in the window. They stared at one another for a long moment, and Dad raised his hand, held it up like a pistol and gestured as though he was shooting Dave.

It didn't scare Dave in the slightest, but I knew how crazy Dad could be, so I shouted, "Ignore him; I'll try talking to him some other day."

Dave did as I said and followed me into my house instead, where I started packing. I had decided to take myself out of Dad's clutches once and for all, and had booked a removal company to arrive that same day. I do actually think that my decisiveness worked as some kind of comfort in that moment, and that it was part of the reason why, when Dave and I drove back to Dad's the next day, I was the one who knocked on the door while Dave waited in the car. This time, he answered. I walked past him without saying a word and sat down at the kitchen table. Dad sloped in after me and didn't look particularly cocky as he sat down on the other side of the table. In fact, he avoided looking me in the eye, and my anger suddenly vanished. All I felt was bottomless sadness.

"Dad, I want you to give me access to all of my accounts and everything to do with my business. And I also want you to apologize for what happened here yesterday."

He cleared his throat as though he was about to say something, but instead he began to cry. It sounded like he was trying to say a few words, but his sobs took over every time. I didn't speak; I just sat there looking at him.

"I'm sorry," he eventually said between sobs, still not looking at me. "Really, really sorry. I love you so much and don't wanna lose you like I lost your Mum."

There was a part of me that wanted to give him another chance, but a stronger voice told me that I had already forgiven him far too often as it was. Just like me and every other adult in this world, he was going to have to take responsibility for his actions and live with the fact that he had lost if not my love, then at least my trust.

"Dad, I'm sad, too," I said, "but this isn't working anymore. You're always drunk or high whenever we go away anywhere, and then I have to take care of everything. You're hardly ever in the office when I need you there. It can't go on like this, and I don't have the energy to keep hoping you'll change."

He buried his face in his hands and started to cry so violently that his whole body shook.

I waited until he had calmed down slightly; then I got up from the table, repeated that I wanted the bank details and everything else, and left his house for the last time.

It really wasn't easy having to suddenly take control of the business side of things. Dad had looked after everything for years, after all, and even now, he didn't seem to want to give it up—despite me having very clearly explained that he was no longer my manager.

Things didn't get any easier when one of the country's most respected papers included me in a list of the UK's richest women, something that piqued the interest of the tax authorities, leading them to begin a comprehensive audit.

If I'm completely honest, I myself was surprised at being named a multimillionaire, because I hadn't exactly been living some kind of luxury lifestyle. I mean, Dad had held the purse strings all along.

In any case, I was called in to Her Majesty's Revenue and Customs for an interview, and there was a real sinking feeling in my stomach when two bureaucrats with serious faces came out to meet me in reception.

I followed them into a plain, fairly cramped meeting room with bright strip lighting, and sat down opposite them on a wooden chair. One of the men looked me straight in the eye and said, "You haven't paid any tax since 1988."

"What?!'"I said, genuinely as shocked as I sounded. "That can't be right. My dad has been managing that for me all these years."

"'Managing' probably isn't the right word," the tax man said. "Actually, he has been seriously mismanaging your taxes for years and has been served rather large fines for doing so."

"Seriously?" I said, feeling the floor practically sway beneath my feet as I continued. "Whenever I've asked him about my taxes, he always reassured me that everything was in order."

The tax man smirked slightly mockingly and didn't seem to care what I had to say.

"Now I want you to tell me which offshore accounts you've hidden the money in. We've managed to link at least twenty-eight different accounts to you, and we're sure there are more."

I felt sick. My mouth was overproducing saliva and I was afraid I would start vomiting at any moment.

"I have no idea what you're talking about," I eventually managed.

"We think you do," the tax man said. "You and your father have arranged it all."

"How are we meant to have done that when we don't even speak anymore?"

"Oh, don't lie," he said, in a harsher tone this time. "You've made up this entire story about the argument with your father. In actual fact, you know all too well where the money is. You're just trying to hide it."

"That's not true," I said, starting to cry. In truth, I did know about one offshore account, because when Peter Foster had paid me for promoting his Bai Lin tea, the money had been deposited into an account in Jersey. But Dad was the one who had looked after both the account and the transaction, and even if that might seem naive with hindsight, I had just trusted that he was following the rules and regulations. I mean, why would he want to hurt or deceive his own daughter? The whole thing seemed inconceivable.

At that moment, an image of the day Dad came home with a bottle of champagne popped into my head. He said, "It's time to celebrate, Sam, because you've just become a millionaire!"

"What, have I?" I had shouted, surprised.

But now, in the harsh glow of the strip lights and with the two men staring at me, I realized how strange that might seem. At the same time, no outsider would ever understand just how close Dad and I had been in the past, nor how strong my trust in him was. For a long time, it had been Dad and me against the world.

"I don't know where the money is," I mumbled, using my fingers to wipe away the mascara that was running down my cheek.

"Here," said the other man, handing me a clean tissue. "You need to realize that we aren't primarily out to get you. We just want to get to the bottom of the tangle your father has managed to create, and we need your help."

I knew they were trying the good cop/bad cop approach with me, but it wasn't going to work. I had no information to give them.

Despite that, I was interviewed several times, and it didn't take long for the bigger picture to start to emerge—not least when my lawyer managed to gain access to the papers that Dad had been trying to conceal. What eventually came to light broke my heart.

It turned out that Dad had been systematically cheating me out of money for some time. He might, for example, tell me that I was being paid ten thousand pounds for a gig, when in actual fact the fee was double that. He and the booking agent would then take five thousand apiece and pocket it themselves. Another example was the house I bought in Spain. Dad had told me a figure that was considerably higher than the asking price, and then kept the difference. He had been embezzling money like that, and I had been none the wiser. The fact that he'd probably used the majority of it to finance his drug and drink habit was hardly any comfort. Somehow, it made the whole thing worse.

But no matter how much I protested that I really had been oblivious to Dad's dodgy dealings with my earnings, the tax authorities refused to believe me. Above all, they couldn't believe that I had signed all those papers Dad had given me without first reading them through. "No one is that gullible," they said. Instead, they were convinced that Dad and I had agreed to blame one another. They started talking about trials, and I was terrified I would end up in jail. Partly, I was afraid of the prison environment itself, but partly I couldn't even imagine the shame.

On my lawyer's recommendation—but also in an attempt to rebuild my own self-respect—I sued Dad for a million pounds. I had finally realized that there was no other way to make him give back what he had stolen from me.

I also tried to liquidate the company that Dad and I had started together, Samantha Fox Ltd—something that proved easier said than done, given that Dad chose to stick his head in the sand and never turn up to the various meetings with lawyers that we'd scheduled. The whole thing cost me a lot of money—money that, in fact, was no longer even mine, since HMRC was now demanding that I pay back everything Dad had withheld from them. The stress and anxiety of it all seriously threatened to devour me, and I went from being someone who had previously never had any trouble sleeping to lying awake all night.

When Dad went to the press and told a whole pack of lies about Mum, who had finally decided to ask for a divorce, I felt like I was literally about to go under.

22

KNIGHT IN SHINING ARMOR

Before the tax men could try to make him leave, he had pulled out a stack of papers from a briefcase and, with a triumphant smile in my direction, said, "Here are all the papers to prove that Sam is telling the truth."

One morning in early summer 1993, when I sat down to eat breakfast with the newspapers in front of me, I got such a shock that I almost knocked over my cup of tea. Splashed across the front page was a picture of Peter Foster, beneath a headline that said, "I'm Going to Marry Samantha Fox."

I had received a number of love messages from Peter through my lawyer, in which he swore that he had never sold me out to the papers and that he still loved me. I read in the paper that he was back in England and determined to marry me, and I couldn't help but think that maybe he had finally lost the plot.

But in actual fact, when he phoned me a day or two later, he sounded completely normal—or rather, just like his usual self. It turned out that Peter had been reading about both my falling out with Dad and the dirt he had been throwing at Mum during their divorce proceedings in the Australian papers, and that it had upset him. It felt good to know that he cared, of course, and he came out with what sounded like a generous suggestion: "I thought I could help you release your new record, because I also read that you were on the lookout for a label."

That was true, because I had sort of lost touch with the record industry after my two deals fell through, and I didn't quite have enough confidence to call any labels myself.

"So if I put up fifty thousand pounds, you'd have enough money to hire a studio, musicians, and a producer," Peter said, "and then you and I would start a label where we each owned 50 percent. I even had an idea for a name: Alchemy. If you want, I can send a draft contract over."

My mind was spinning. I just didn't know what to think, and things didn't get any less strange when I went back to the tax authorities the next day. As I sat there, staring helplessly at the stack of the papers I had evidently signed, Peter suddenly stormed into the room in that self-confident way only he could.

Before the tax men could try to make him leave, he had pulled out a stack of papers from a briefcase and, with a triumphant smile in my direction, said, "Here are all the papers to prove that Sam is telling the truth."

He had receipts for everything he had bought for me, for example, but more importantly he also had the details of the offshore account Dad had used to hide money. That was where Peter had transferred all of the payments for the promotional work I'd done for his weight-loss tea.

But that was hardly the end of the saga. Only a week or two later, he was my knight in shining armor once again—this time in court, where Mum and Dad were at war through their legal representatives. Dad had told Mum that she wouldn't be getting a penny from him, and he had stood up in court and claimed that she owned a number of expensive items—things like Cartier watches, Mercedes cars, and jewelry, which in actual fact Peter had bought for me, not her. But, once again, Peter had turned up completely unannounced, and he said, "I have all the receipts to prove that those things belong to Sam, not Carole."

The female judge asked to see the receipts, and, after studying them for a while, focused her gaze on Dad and said, "Patrick Fox, you have demonstrably lied to the court and consequently lack credibility."

She ruled in Mum's favor and ordered Dad to pay all of the legal costs. When she struck her gavel on the desk, I saw Dad slump in his seat next to his lawyer. It was as though, in the space of just a few seconds, the past had finally caught up with him, dealing him the blow that would finally sink him.

Not long after that, I was forced to go through another court case, this time about the business Dad and I shared. The whole thing was really awful. I mean, in a sense, we were all losers. The fact that Dad was ordered to pay what was left of the money he had stashed away in Jersey back to me was hardly any consolation, since I still owed the tax authorities almost a million pounds. They took everything I had and forced me to sell the flat in Spain in under a week, for such a low price that I made absolutely no money from the sale. They also added interest for all the years Dad hadn't bothered paying my taxes. All in all, it bankrupted me.

I remember lying in bed at Mum and Colin's house on one of those days, staring up at the ceiling. The house was completely silent, since Mum was at work. Had it all been in vain? Right then, that was how it felt. But I also knew that I had no choice but to keep going. I mean, I'd started out empty-handed at one point in time, and I could do the same again. So, a few weeks later, I started calling various booking agents, putting on a voice and telling them that my name was Karen Fuller and that I was Samantha Fox's manager. People thought I was related to Simon Fuller, the Spice Girls' manager! I even had business cards printed with that name on them. Before long, I was booked to play a number of gigs in Russia. That in turn meant I was soon able to buy a small flat on Truro Road, just two minutes' walk from my old secondary school and close to the park bench where I smoked my first cigarette.

It was around this time that I got to know an agent called Debbie Haxton, and I happened to show her the draft contract Peter had given me. It only took her a few minutes to realize that it looked dodgy, and though my options were limited, I decided not to go into business with him.

But though what Debbie said had once again put me on my guard when it came to Peter, I was still flattered that he had come charging to my rescue like he had, and by summer 1993 we were dating again. He was still adamant that he was going to marry me, though I wasn't the least bit interested in that. I wasn't interested in marketing the cellulite cream he wanted to launch, either. When I told him that, I remember he asked me who the "nineties Samantha Fox" was.

"Pamela Anderson," I told him.

"I'll ask her instead, then," he said.

Good luck, I thought. But to my surprise, he really did manage to get her to appear in his ad campaign. Peter was incredibly good at getting people involved in his various business projects, only to then mess things up for himself.

At a party around this time, I found out from a friend that Peter had also convinced a page three girl called Maria Whittaker to promote his cellulite cream. When I read about another girl who had marketed Peter's products in one of the big papers—and who claimed to have been in some kind of relationship with him. Regardless of whether it was true or not, it was the final straw for me. Suddenly, I could see a clear pattern in Peter's behavior towards me over the years. The feeling of having essentially been used was so strong that I called him up that very same day and told him I didn't want to see him anymore—ever.

Working was one good way of keeping my mind busy after that, and just a month or so later, I got on a plane to Bosnia—which was experiencing a full-blown civil war at the time—to entertain the British UN troops. *The Sun* had asked me to deliver letters from their loved ones, as they needed something else to think about for a while, too. Sadly, the experience was a little too adventurous for my liking, because during my transfer from the airport in an armored jeep, we suddenly heard swishing and popping sounds, and my driver immediately shouted, "Get on the floor!"

I threw myself down and heard something hit the windscreen, which—thankfully—was bulletproof. It turned out that snipers had been firing at us, and as I lay there on the floor with my bum in the air, I felt more exposed than ever before. My heart was galloping in my chest and strange thoughts started rushing through my mind: *If I take a bullet now, just let it be in an arm or a leg.*

My backside was the part of me sticking up most, but suddenly it also felt like the part of me most worthy of protection. So I tore off the helmet I had been given by the driver and held it over my bum.

Afterwards, I felt slightly ashamed at what I had done, but I soon had other things to worry about; the troops took me on a helicopter ride to show me what war was really like.

We landed in a village that seemed to be completely deserted. It had, they told me, been the scene of ethnic cleansing, and they took me to a house that was completely blown out. Someone had put a bomb by the front door, knocked, and then run away. Right next to the gaping hole where the door once stood, I could see a child's shoe.

"How are we meant to make sense of these people, who have lived next to one another for years and years, suddenly starting to slaughter one another?" the sergeant standing next to me asked.

But there was no making sense of it.

My own problems suddenly seemed if not meaningless then at least entirely manageable in comparison to what I saw in those war-torn villages. It was so much to process that even after I flew on to Estonia to do an outdoor gig in Tallinn, my mind was still in Bosnia. The free concert was part of a street festival that had been arranged to celebrate Estonia's newfound independence from the Soviet Union. A stage had been built at a crossroads in the middle of the city, and as I stepped up onto it, there were people as far as the eye could see in every direction.

My drummer, John Tonkin, had previously told me that while he was on tour with Bonnie Tyler, he used to let her know if she had said something wrong using his bass drum. Once, she had stepped from a plane in South Africa and said to the press, "I'm so pleased to be in Australia!" John hadn't been sitting behind his drums at the time, and he'd had to whisper loudly instead, "Bom bom!"

So, when I opened our gig in Tallinn with the words "Good evening, Russia!" it was followed by a sudden thundering from John's bass drum.

23

CHRISSIE BONACCI

"You don't love me!" she would scream
over and over again.

It was only really in spring 1994 that I finally had a clear enough grip of my finances to buy a small three-bedroom house in Finchley. It felt great to finally have a real home of my own, but at the same time, I was still upset and confused over Dad's betrayal. It wasn't that I thought about it every single day, but it would occasionally overwhelm me with such force that I didn't know where to turn. I was making a workout DVD with the Irish boxer Barry McGuigan around this time, and one day as I was having my makeup done, the makeup artist suddenly turned to me and said, "You have a lot of sorrow in your eyes." She said it with such sincerity that I felt the tears stinging my eyes almost immediately. And though I didn't know her at all, I heard myself telling her everything that had happened. She listened without either commenting or interrupting, and only once I was finished did she say, "I know a great evangelical church in Knightsbridge. I think you'd like it. It's easy to talk to people there."

By that point, I was willing to try almost anything, and so a few days later, I found myself heading over there. All I can say is that the makeup artist was right: it really was easy to talk to people there.

The first person I met was the man who led the congregation. His name was Jerry, and I told him how angry and disappointed I sometimes felt with Dad, not just because he had stolen my money but also because he had stopped me from being able to trust anyone. Jerry didn't say or do much right there and then, but later that day, he asked the entire congregation to pray for me, and I've never experienced anything else like it. We stood there together in the middle of the church, and, as though on command, the members of the congregation laid their hands on me as they said their prayers. To begin with, it felt like I was filled with some kind of joy, but then I began to sob. Jerry said that the reason I was crying was that I had received the holy spirit—and I know it sounds odd, but it really did feel like I had taken a step upwards and left not only my body but all kinds of suffering on the church floor beneath me.

Not long after that, I began a so-called alpha course at a church called Holy Trinity Brompton. I also started going to prayer meetings once a week. It was nothing like the church I was used to from my childhood. Instead, it was full of young, trendy people who, among other things, sang good, modern music with lyrics that dealt with important issues. The priest also dressed in a modern way and talked about life in terms that felt real. No matter how much or how little I believed in God, just being there made me feel good. Sadly, however, the press caught wind of it and wrote that I had become a bible basher, and suddenly there would be paparazzi waiting for me every time I left the church. It assumed such absurd proportions that eventually, I no longer had the energy to keep going.

After everything that had happened with Dad, I'd had a number of different managers. At that particular moment, I was being represented by a woman called Debbie Haxton—the one who had exposed Peter's draft contract as a bluff. She was also the one who introduced me to Chrissie Bonacci, the guitarist from Girl School.

Chrissie was tired of touring and had, during this period, started dreaming about becoming a music producer. For my own part, I was writing more songs than ever, and when Chrissie told me that she had broken up with her girlfriend and had nowhere to live, I told her she could move into my guest room, above the office on the ground floor. A few weeks later, when she did just that, it was the start of a very creative period in my life.

We recorded several of my songs and also wrote a number of new ones together. She even started coming to gigs with me, as my guitarist. It was through the music that we found one another, and eventually it led to us falling in love.

Chrissie came from a fairly strict Italian family and still hadn't come out as gay by that point in time. For the reasons I mentioned earlier, I was also keen for no one to know, and so we decided to keep our relationship a secret. The fact that we worked together meant it was possible.

It didn't take long before we started to build a studio in my house. Or, more accurately, I spent almost fifty thousand quid on some studio equipment and got two guys to build me a soundproofed room in which, over the next seven months, we would record my entire next album. It would be given the name *21st Century Fox*.

One day around this time, I got a very strange phone call from Debbie.

"I got a fax," she said, "and I think it's from your dad."

It was morning, and I was in the kitchen making coffee for Chrissie and myself.

"But," Debbie continued, "obviously I'm not 100 percent sure it's from him. It could just be some fan mucking around."

She wasn't wrong there. I mean, I still have fans who call themselves Patrick Fox. I've even received letters from Patrick Fox since Dad died. Strange letters, to say the least. Some fans have even changed their names to Sam Fox.

In any case, Debbie said that Dad—if it was him—had written to say he had been trying to get in touch, and that he really needed to see me. There was so much he needed to talk about with me, he said, and then he had signed off with "Kind regards, Mr. Patrick Fox."

Debbie knew all about what had happened with Dad, and she asked me what I wanted to do. If I'm honest, over the years that had passed, I'd always had the vague hope that Dad and I would be able to meet and he would say sorry so we could try and repair our relationship. So, after lots of umm-ing and ahh-ing, I decided to take a chance and dialed the number Debbie had been given . . . even though I was still agonizing about it while I did so. The hand holding the receiver was sticky with sweat, and I remember hesitating as I said, "Hi, it's me . . . Sammy."

Dad, on the other hand, sounded as though nothing had happened.

"That's unbelievable, guess what I'm doing?"

"Uh . . . I don't know?"

"I'm sitting here with my daughter. You know I have a little daughter now?"

"Yeah," I said, because I had read it in the papers—or, more accurately, I had seen a picture of her and Vanessa there.

"I'm sitting here now, showing her pictures of you."

I didn't really know what to say. The whole thing felt incredibly awkward.

"I'd like to see you . . . Do you think we could meet . . . tomorrow?"

Maybe it's just something I'm just imagining looking back, but I do think that in that moment, a slight hope flickered inside me.

"OK," I said. "Where should we meet?"

Dad immediately sounded even more relaxed, almost happy, when he said, "Do you remember the pub in Crouch End, on the corner, opposite 7-Eleven? You can park there."

"OK, do you want to meet outside, or should we meet inside?"

"Outside."

The next morning, I drove over there a little too early and paced back and forth in the car park for a while before I noticed him sitting inside with a cup of coffee. He looked older, and when he came out to meet me I noticed that he must be having trouble with his back—he could barely get into my new car, which was really small and low.

"Where are we going?" I asked.

"What about a coffee in Muswell Hill?" he said, giving me a questioning look.

I felt uncomfortable having to drive with him next to me, because while I was learning to drive as a teenager, he would always criticize me and make me feel incredibly stressed.

All the same, I also felt very grown up, sitting there in a car I had bought with my own money.

We managed to find a near-empty café in Muswell Hill, and after our coffees arrived and we made small talk for a while, I felt myself relax. I was having a good time. Or I was until Dad got down to the real reason he'd wanted to meet.

"I've been offered book deals about how I made you," he said, holding up his hands.

Back then, I had never even considered writing a book, despite having been offered large sums of money to do just that.

"Since our breakup, the press has gone crazy . . . they're all after me for my story."

I didn't know what to say, so I just sat there and stared at him. I didn't quite want to believe what I was hearing. Dad hadn't wanted to meet to say sorry or attempt to straighten anything out; it was so he would have a happy ending for his book. Which is what he himself said: "Can you imagine how fantastic it feels to be able to write that we've found our way back to one another and put all that shit behind us? That we're a family again."

I still didn't say anything, but Dad didn't seem bothered by my silence. He continued to talk about how he had also been offered movie deals and how our story would make a fantastic film now that we were solid again.

Thankfully, none of it ever actually came off. Partly because Dad was in far too bad a shape to be able to handle any kind of project, and partly because no one was likely to believe a single word he wrote.

By early autumn, the record Chrissie and I had been working on was finally finished, and Jonathan King, whom I still saw relatively often, had booked me a meeting with Simon Cowell, to see whether he might be interested in releasing it. Simon had just had several hits with Robson & Jerome, two celebrities who sang cover versions, and when we met at his office, he said, "You're a household name. I actually think you're the same kind of artist as Robson & Jerome. You should do a covers record."

It wasn't exactly what I had been hoping to hear. I mean, I'd just spent a good deal of time and money on writing, producing, and recording that album. So I said no. Instead, I started thinking of alternative ways of launching my record, and when I went to see Mum one day, I played her "Go for the Heart"—a song I'd written with my bassist and music director, Jonathan Durno.

"That'd be a good fit for Eurovision," Mum hooted right after the very first chorus.

I had never seen myself as that kind of artist, but now that Mum had said it, I realized the song really could work in the Eurovision Song Contest. A few weeks later, I submitted it anonymously, and by the turn of the year, I found out that I was one of the finalists. People were surprised, to say the least, which resulted in quite a lot being written in the British papers. If I'm honest, I was quite surprised, too, because although I obviously liked the song, I hadn't made any plans to take part in the program. I remember talking about it quite a bit with Chrissie, and after bouncing ideas back and forth with our friend Lorraine McIntosh, we decided to enter the competition as a band.

We called ourselves Sox and finished fourth in the UK finals.

Working like that, with my girlfriend, really was fantastic. But at the same time, I could see a number of tendencies I recognized from my earlier relationships with men. Chrissie still seemed to have strong ties to her ex and even continued to pay all of her bills. Whenever she spoke to her on the phone, she would close the door behind her. But it wasn't so much that which felt familiar as the insecurity that started to rear its head. In terms of both jealousy and a need to be in control, women can obviously be just as crazy as men. Women can also be just as dangerous as men—if not more so. But Chrissie wasn't dangerous, just incredibly insecure. She really didn't believe that I loved her, and on those occasions when I didn't feel like having sex, she would interpret it as proof.

"You don't love me!" she would scream over and over again.

24

PLAYBOY

I'm just happy and proud that I have been
able to bring happiness to so many men.

During the second half of the nineties, the number of gigs started to dry up. Instead, I started getting quite a few different job offers. *Playboy* had contacted me countless times during the eighties, desperate to do a foldout, but it was only as my thirtieth birthday approached that I finally decided to say yes. I mean, I was now old enough to know what I wanted, and one of my demands was that I could choose both the photographer and the location myself. I also got full picture and copy approval to make sure the photos were tasteful.

In the end, it was Byron Newman behind the camera, and the location was St. Barts in the West Indies. Just like in the good old days, Mum came along to make sure that everything went to plan. I remember studying a couple of foldout shoots that Pamela Anderson had done, where she showed more of her bum than her breasts, and I also remember Mum shouting that to the photographer as he snapped away: "Come on, Byron, take some bum shots, too!"

Though maybe she shouldn't have, because Byron always took photos from such low angles that you could see much more than just my bum. And yes, I'm just happy and proud that I have been able to bring happiness to so many men for so many years, but I've also always known where to draw the line. As has Mum, who now interrupted.

"Lift it up a bit please, Byron! It's a bit low," she said to him in her usual friendly but firm way.

Sadly, it didn't help. As always before that type of shoot, I had been sunbathing nude, and a couple of paparazzi circling overhead in helicopters had taken pictures that would soon be published across the world.

There were fewer gigs during this period, like I said, but one I do remember particularly well was at a huge gasworks in Siberia. I mean, imagine being part of a group of men who have worked together for four or five months without seeing their wives, still not earning all that much, and then having me turn up like a jack-in-the-box to sing for them. In situations like that, being an artist is a lot of fun, even if the practical circumstances of that particular gig weren't the best.

It was me, Chrissie, two dancers, Tina—who worked with my new management team—and a journalist and photographer from *Cosmopolitan* magazine, which was running a longer piece on the whole thing. They really must have gotten a good story out of it, because things started to go wrong almost the minute we landed in Russia. There was a snowstorm outside, and it was freezing cold. The house we were staying in was in the middle of nowhere, and we were forced to make the last part of the journey in a military helicopter. When we eventually arrived, the little house was at least warm, but that's probably the only positive thing I have to say about it. In every other respect, it was actually pretty awful. There were so many cockroaches there that when we turned out the lights that evening, you could hear them scuttling about inside the walls.

"I can't sleep with that noise in my ears," Chrissie sighed. Not long after that, we heard the two dancers shouting from another room, "What is this!? I'm dying!"

In the end, we all left our bedrooms and lay down next to one another on the floor in the hallway. Just before I fell asleep, I heard Chrissie say, "At least we only have to spend one night here."

I wholeheartedly agreed. The only problem was that when we woke the next morning, we realized we had been snowed in. So we were forced to spend two more nights with the cockroaches before we could finally leave to do the show—which, despite everything, was a real success.

Not long after that, the girls and I were due to play another gig, and again we were forced to finish off our journey in a helicopter—this time because the show was in a small town in northern Norway. I'm not especially scared of flying. I mean, I've flown in private Russian planes without seatbelts, toured in Lebanon as the bombs fell around us, performed with tanks to the side of the stage, and been told to move as much as possible to avoid being hit by snipers. But on this particular occasion, we would be flying over a glacier, and throughout the entire journey north, it was fantastic to be able to look down at the beautiful, dramatic landscape. The gig went well, too. But the return journey was very different. We had been up in the air for some time when a snowstorm suddenly appeared from nowhere. We were right above the glacier at the time, and we were all wearing headphones with microphones, meaning I could both see and hear the pilot's state of panic.

"I need to go down until I can see the fjord!" he practically screamed.

There were high mountains on either side of us, but we could no longer see them, and our only chance of making it was somehow following the fjord below. Shortly afterwards, I heard the pilot talking to a ferry that was apparently directly beneath us.

"I'm on my way down to you," he said. "I have Samantha Fox on board."

At that very moment, Kathryn, one of my dancers, suddenly started screaming into the microphone at the top of her lungs. She'd had some kind of breakdown, and wouldn't tour with me again for several years. In a way, I do understand her; I could feel my own heart pounding in my chest, felt the cold sweat, even if I didn't say anything at the time.

In any case, we soon saw the ferry beneath us. News that I was on board the helicopter must have spread quickly among the passengers, because we saw people coming out on deck to wave to me.

We were hovering directly above the ferry now, and the helicopter was still swaying from side to side, but we no longer had to worry that we were about to crash into a mountainside. Still, Kathryn continued to scream into her microphone, and did so until we found a field we could land in.

We climbed out of the helicopter on shaking legs, and I hardly need to say how good it felt to have solid ground beneath my feet. There was a small farm a few hundred yards away, and we saw two people come running towards us out of the house.

It was the farmer and his wife; both had kind eyes and both seemed to be in their fifties.

"Are you OK?"

The pilot gave them a quick summary of what had happened, and the woman told us to follow her inside.

It was just before Easter, and once we were all sitting down in their kitchen, the farmer's wife served us waffles with jam and cream.

The pair had a son, and when he and his girlfriend came to eat, he was so shocked to see me there that he could barely say a word. It turned out he was a huge fan and had posters of me all over his room, so our emergency landing in his field must have seemed completely surreal to him.

In any case, the farm was a sheep farm, and the girls and I went out to see a lamb being born, which was fantastic. I mean, I'm a North London girl, so I had never seen anything like it, but then I found out that they were planning to eat that particular lamb for Easter. I think it was the farmer who mentioned it. I thought the whole thing sounded completely awful, so I shouted, "No, you can't eat it!"

The farmer just looked at me and sighed, but he did at least promise he would spare the lamb and call it Sam.

It was a ram, and for years after that, he would appear in the local paper on his birthday. They made a big deal of the fact that he had only lived because of me.

Shortly after this, we started to talk about how we were going to get out of there. I remember we called for a taxi, but since so many cars had crashed or gotten caught up in the snow, no one could or would drive us. We were up in the mountains, after all, and I could just see how we might end up getting stuck there for a week.

"So, what do you think?" the pilot asked after a while. "Do you want to risk flying, or should we ask if we can spend the night here?"

Though the family was kind and friendly in every way, we really did want to leave as soon as we could. Not least because I was booked to play a gig at a nightclub in Barcelona that evening.

"Let's risk it," I said.

"OK, we'll wait a while and hope the weather gets a bit better. Then we go."

After that, he went out to check the weather at regular intervals, and a few hours later he suddenly came back in and said, "It's cleared up. Let's get going."

Though the flight was bumpy, the visibility was much better, and we made it to the airport in Stavanger without further incident. We even managed to catch the last scheduled flight to Amsterdam, where we flew on to Barcelona. It meant we could do the gig as planned, at four in the morning, to a fully packed club in the very center of town.

During these years, I started getting more and more requests from authors who were interested in writing my biography. The first to contact me was a woman who worked for the *Sunday People*. It must have been autumn 1998, and I remember that after our first meeting, I went to her house in Islington, where we spent the whole day working on a synopsis. The problem was that I quickly realized she was really only interested in all of the bad things that had happened in my life.

As observant readers will no doubt have noticed by now, I have nothing against talking about that kind of thing; it's just that it needs to be done with a certain amount of humor. I mean, black is rarely just black and white is rarely just white. But this woman was very much like a journalist in her approach to my story, and we didn't really strike up the kind of rapport I was looking for. She noticed and got annoyed, which made me even more hesitant, and I started saying things like, "Yeah, maybe . . . I'm not sure . . ."

In the end, she asked whether I wanted a drink. I replied that a glass of wine would be nice. She didn't have any wine, only vodka, so I said, "A small vodka and orange," as it was OK to have one drink and still drive. But rather than pouring me a single measure of vodka, she must have poured at least three and mixed it with Coca-Cola so I couldn't tell how strong it was. I also hadn't eaten a thing.

A while later, as I was about to leave, she called both the *Sunday People* and the police, meaning they were all waiting outside my house when I got home. At first, I didn't understand what was going on. There were two police cars there, and the officers handcuffed me almost as soon as I stepped out of my car. I really needed to pee, and I asked to go to the toilet.

"Lay off it," was all they said, shoving me into the back of the police car.

"Can you at least take these off? They hurt," I said, nodding towards the handcuffs. "It's not like I'm planning on doing anything."

But they were incredibly unkind towards me, and said, "Don't think you'll get any special treatment just because you're Samantha Fox."

Naturally, the news picked up the story. I had gone straight from that woman's house in Islington to my place in Finchley, but the TV news had driven a car that looked like mine, and they had filmed it. Only I hadn't driven the route they showed—on the

North Circular Road. I'd headed straight to Holloway Road, through Highgate and onto East Finchley. One straight road. My driving license was taken away for a year.

That winter, Chrissie and I were going through a really bad phase. Her jealousy had started to turn her into someone even she could barely stand.

I had a friend during this time who knew everyone and everything, who lived in Primrose Hill and who, on New Year's Eve 1998, had invited the two of us to a party. I realized that Chrissie wasn't in the mood to party, or even do anything fun, while we were still getting ready at home. She spent the entire evening at my friend's house being more withdrawn than usual, and wanted to leave immediately after midnight.

"Come on, let's go," she said, grabbing my arm.

I shook my head. I knew that All Saints were coming to the party, and I wanted to meet them. Or . . . I mainly wanted to meet Nicole. I had heard she was upset that she was no longer allowed to write her own material for All Saints. I also knew that Nicole was with Robbie Williams, and I saw the chance of being able to work with interesting people. I tried to explain all this in a whisper to Chrissie, but even under ordinary circumstances, she wasn't someone who looked to the future—she was more someone who went about life just waiting for things to happen. She was also feeling jealous and blue. So she just gave me an angry look and left.

Two hours later, Nicole arrived, and we immediately clicked when we started talking.

"I just write lyrics," she said, "can't write music, but I'm really good at lyrics."

"Well, I write music and can arrange songs, and would love to do something with you if you'd give me some lyrics," I said.

To my surprise, she took a scrap of paper from her pocket and handed it to me. It was more a poem than anything, but I told her I could turn it into a song by splitting the text into blocks.

I remember how happy I felt about it all, and we got to work on the song the very next day. But New Year's Day also began with a good deal of jealousy.

Chrissie was angrier than I had ever seen her before, and shouted that I had only stayed at the party so I could get with Nicole. No matter what I said, it only seemed to prove that fact to her. Eventually, I didn't have the energy to argue anymore; I just eagerly awaited Nicole's arrival instead. We had agreed for her to come over at three-ish, and at half past two, the phone rang. It was Robbie Williams.

"Hi," he said, his voice sounding almost anxious. "Nicole and I were going to come over now, but I just wanted to make sure you didn't have any drugs or booze at your home."

To begin with, I thought he was joking, but the other end of the line was silent, so I said, "Nope, you don't have to worry, there's not a single one here."

They turned up a while later, and that same evening, Nicole and I really did write a song together. We called it "Dreams." Nicole sang it through in the studio, and Robbie added backing vocals. All Saints would later release the song on one of their records, and it would be produced by William Orbit—who, apparently, loved it.

Nicole and I went for a fifty-fifty split, which felt fair. But it turned out that she didn't want my name on the record. I thought about it for a while and eventually decided to go along with what she wanted. In the end, I used Mum's maiden name, Wilkins, which is what appears in the credits. I earned about sixty thousand pounds from the song, so maybe it was worth it after all.

Anyway, it was around seven in the morning when we finally finished the recording. Chrissie and I had collapsed into bed upstairs, and Nicole and Robbie were waiting for a taxi downstairs. Suddenly, Robbie burst into my room, where Chrissie and I were naked together in bed.

"Sam!" he said, his jaw almost dropping when he saw us. "Do you have a cap or something I can use to cover my face? I have to go out to the taxi."

25

MYRA

In many ways, she was a strong woman. I'm the same:
tough on the surface, but weak as anything in my heart.

Our paths really should have crossed much sooner. She grew up on
Brecknock Road in Islington, just a stone's throw from Morgan
Mansions. Her dad rented a pub there, which was next door to the
house where my aunt Maureen lived. We also had several friends in
common and moved in vaguely the same circles. But still, it wasn't
until I started shooting a film called *The Match* that I heard her
name for the first time.

Neil Morrissey, one of the other actors in the film, used to come
over to chat with me during breaks in filming. On one occasion, I
mentioned that I was looking for a new manager. Neil must have
given it some thought, because he came back to me a few days later
and said, "I know someone who could be great for you. Her name is
Myra Stratton, and she's a Sharon Osbourne type. But she decided
she'd had enough of the music industry, and she does various theatre
productions now. She looks after the financing and things like that,
so I don't even know if she'd be interested in going back, but she'd
definitely suit you."

A few months later, in autumn 1999, I met up with another author
who was interested in working with me on my autobiography. Her
name was Jane Owen, and among other things, she had written a

book called *Camden Girls*. My accountant was the one who had first put us in touch, and I had gone along with at least meeting her, at her flat in Camden.

I remember that she had made sandwiches and that she suggested we eat and get to know one another better before we started talking work. Suddenly, she put her hand to her forehead and said, "You'll have to excuse me, I've got such a bad hangover today."

"No problem," I laughed. "Late night?"

"VERY late . . . I drank a load of tequila with my friend Neil Morrissey and another friend called Myra Stratton."

That set off a bell ringing in my head, and I asked whether this Myra was also a manager. It turned out she was the same person Neil had mentioned, and that she also lived in Hampstead, not far from Jane.

"What do you think about ringing her and asking her to come over for a drink?"

"Sure . . . why not," Jane grinned. And, an hour or so later, I phoned Myra myself. She had been on my mind, as I knew she was gay.

"Hi, this is Samantha Fox."

There was silence at the other end of the line, and then I heard her take a deep breath.

"And . . ."

"I'm sitting here with Jane, writing a synopsis for my autobiography, and we wondered whether you wanted to come over. We were planning to open a bottle of champagne. Jane's cooking pasta . . . and . . ."

"Listen, if you want a meeting, you'll have to grab everything and come over here."

I loved that attitude—she was cheeky—so after Jane and I had shared the bottle of champagne, we jumped into a taxi and were standing outside the building where Myra lived just a few minutes later. She had been living there since she had broken up with her girlfriend—she had just left and moved out. For my part, I had broken up with Chrissie relatively recently, and she had taken practically all of the studio equipment I had bought while I was away on a trip. In any case, I was struck by Myra's charisma the minute she opened the door. I don't really know how to explain it, but it was like my entire being vanished in her gaze. Much later, she would tell me that she had felt the same—or rather that she'd thought: *Oh, no, I'm in trouble.* Despite the fact I wasn't wearing any makeup that evening, and was dressed in a tracksuit and cap.

Jane and I had bought a bottle of champagne en route, but I didn't dare hand it over to Myra because her dog scared the shit out of me. Jane must have realized how scared I was, because she took the bottle out of my hand and handed it to Myra, who invited us in.

Her dog was an American Staffordshire terrier. It looked scary, and unfortunately dog fighters had given that breed a bad name. It stared at me the whole time, growling and baring its teeth. I was used to cute little fluffy lapdogs, so I really found it unnerving. But I quickly got used to it, and by the end of the evening, I found myself sitting on the floor and playing with it.

Aside from the fact that Myra had such a natural authority and charisma, I liked that she had no idea about page three or my career in general, and when my songs came up in conversation, she just said that she wasn't interested in that kind of music.

We really did find one another right there and then, and I stayed until just after three in the morning. By the time I left, I had a strong sense that Myra and I had been meant to meet.

As far as Jane and the autobiography were concerned, I actually turned her down, purely because it didn't feel right again.

Just a few days later, Myra and I had a proper business meeting, and we decided that she would be my manager. We really tried to be professional about it, but at the same time, the sparks were flying between us, and she quickly became someone I looked up to, someone I felt safe around. Without making a big deal of it, Myra was there for me, and she looked after my interests. In many ways, she was a strong woman. I'm the same: tough on the surface, but weak as anything in my heart. (The ex lost her job and took it out on Myra, who, given the circumstances, was extremely generous and considerate.)

In any case, once we got together and Myra stepped in as my manager, we were practically inseparable. We slept together every night, either at my place or hers, and she helped me to work out what I should do next in my career.

"Take a sabbatical year!" she said with a shrug.

I thought I'd misheard her to begin with, so I just stared at her. We were sitting in the living room of her rented flat in Hampstead.

"You've told me how you've been working constantly since you were sixteen, and about everything that's had a negative impact on you over these past few years. You need to regain your strength so that you can focus on writing a really good album and take the time to get to know yourself." This was so caring. She wasn't interested in the money she could earn, just caring about my welfare.

Right then, my phone rang. It was Vanessa, and I didn't have time to do anything but pick up before she said, "Something's happened to Dad."

I felt my entire body freeze. Dad and I hadn't talked in several years, but I knew that he was in a bad way.

"Is it his liver?"

"It's best if you come over; then we can talk."

Shortly after that, Myra and I left for Vanessa's. We barely made it into the hallway before Vanessa said, "Dad's dead."

I stared uncomprehendingly at her.

"My dad's dead?!"

The moment I said it, I saw a hard look appear in Vanessa's eye.

"*Your* dad. It's always about you. '*My* dad's dead'? What about me; isn't he *my* dad, too?"

These were probably just old feelings washing over her. I mean, we both knew that Dad and I had had a special relationship when we were younger, and I assume that had hurt her. But I didn't say anything further, and she didn't, either.

Myra, on the other hand, thought I should go to see Dad.

"It's important, love," she said while we were in the taxi on the way back to her flat. "You need to make your peace with him."

I had never seen a dead person before, and I hadn't seen Dad in six, maybe seven years. But I phoned my sister the next morning anyway, to find out where he was. She told me and said that she had also taken care of everything with regard to the funeral.

"Is he dressed nicely?"

"No, he's wearing a shroud."

I thought it seemed strange, but I didn't say anything. I didn't have the energy to argue with Vanessa again.

When Myra and I went to see Dad that same day, he was at least wearing a suit. But his nails were long and his fingers were yellow from nicotine. His second wife, Janey, left him after he beat her up while he was drunk. He hadn't had anywhere to go, and had ended up in a shelter for homeless people. His pancreas had given up, and they found him in his room—which was full of pictures of me—surrounded by bottles of spirits.

As I stood there looking at him, I thought that if I had only known he was so ill, I would never have let things go so far. Apparently he hadn't eaten in weeks before he died. Vanessa had been to see him a few times, and left food by his bed. I wished that somehow I'd known. Maybe I could have forgiven him and he would be all right to this day. He'd always taken care of his appearance. He used to trim his nose hair each and every day. He moisturized and wore decent suits. He always looked good. So, as I looked at him then, it felt like even in appearance, it was no longer him.

I had written a letter, which I put into his jacket pocket, along with a picture of me wearing no makeup—his Sammy, in other words. I gave him one last kiss on the cheek, and before Myra and I left, I told him that I forgave him.

Then it was time for the funeral. Things between Vanessa and me were very tense, and when we walked into the church, she refused to let Myra sit next to me.

"You didn't know my dad and you don't know my family, so you'll have to go and sit at the back," she said.

Myra didn't want to argue, so she did as she was told. But Pauline, one of my friends, came to sit next to me, which felt good. After all, Vanessa was there with her family, and Dad's new family was there. Mum had chosen not to attend, so it felt like I was all on my own.

Myra and I celebrated Christmas at my house that year. One day, as I was sitting at the table downstairs, wrapping presents for Myra, who was upstairs, I suddenly had the sense that someone was standing next to me. The feeling was so clear that I was terrified. From the corner of one eye, I could see the outline of a figure slowly—almost in slow motion—holding out its arms to me. Then I heard Dad's voice saying, "Sammy, come here."

I didn't dare turn my head, because I wasn't sure I could cope with seeing him again. Still, there was no doubt that it was his voice I was hearing.

I said, "Dad, leave me in peace. You know I can't handle this kind of thing."

Then I got up and hesitantly made my way over to the door. I reached the stairs and rushed up them as quickly as I could.

26

A YEAR OF MAGICAL TRAVEL

There had been plenty of rumors even while I was with Chrissie, and I now found myself frequently being asked about Myra. So, mostly in an attempt to stop all the speculation, I took the leap and told the truth.

Not long after the turn of the millennium, I followed Myra's advice and took a year off.

I hadn't written any songs in a while, and I knew in myself that I needed to take a break if I was going to find some new energy. But first, Myra and I decided to announce to the world that we were a couple.

There had been plenty of rumors even while I was with Chrissie, and I now found myself frequently being asked about Myra. So, mostly in an attempt to stop all the speculation, I took the leap and told the truth. I can honestly say that it felt pretty horrible. But at the same time, it wasn't the eighties anymore, the world was moving forward, and other than a couple of indignant letters from hardcore male fans who'd followed me over the years, people seemed to take it pretty well.

Not long after that, Myra and I began planning a long holiday together. Or, more accurately, we decided to use my year off to travel, and though we had no detailed plans for where we wanted to go or what we wanted to do, we agreed that we'd start in my old neighborhood of New York.

During that time, I slowly but surely began writing songs again, too. Myra said to me, "Write about yourself; use your songs as a way of channeling all the shit that's happened to you these past few years."

So that was exactly what I did, and the result was my most personal album to date: *Angel with an Attitude.*

We really did have a great time in New York, and it gave us the opportunity to get to know one another properly.

I remember realizing, as Myra talked about her childhood and youth, that she had a touch of the rebel inside her, just like me. She'd tried to burn down her school in Woodford, and had been expelled like I had. But, as tough as Myra could be, she was also equally fragile and sensitive—maybe even more so when it came to our relationship. We spent quite a lot of time with my friends from New York while we were there, and I remember one particular evening when we met Celeste and Natalie at a gay bar—I've forgotten which now. In any case, a couple of girls there recognized me and came over to ask for my autograph, which meant that other people also started to notice my presence.

"Come on," said Myra. "We're going."

"Soon," I said, continuing to sign my name for the girls around me.

"Now!" Myra insisted, taking a firm grip of my arm.

Right then, Celeste took a step forward and, in her characteristic New York accent, said, "What the fuck are you doin'?"

Myra and Celeste would later become close friends, but they didn't know one another at that particular point in time, and before I knew it, they were arguing and pushing and shoving.

It turned out that even Myra had her jealous and controlling side. But other than that, being with her felt like coming home, something that became especially clear when we decided to move on to Thailand after New York. It was Jon Astrop (one of the songwriters on "Touch Me," and a close friend of mine) who tipped us off about the island that he and his wife had discovered a few years earlier, and later built a house on.

There were no luxury hotels on the island, barely even any tourists, and no kind of night life to speak of. Maybe that's what made us fall head over heels for the place. I mean, we were staying in a simple, almost spartan bungalow, with the crystal-clear sea just outside our door. Looking back now, I'm glad that we were able to focus so completely on one another, that we got that time together as a couple. After just a few days on the island, we stopped washing our hair and shaving our legs, and by the time a few months had passed, we no longer missed civilization. The truth is, I'd never felt as free before.

In the early 2000s, reality TV shows became big business in England, and though I was booked to play some gigs when we returned home from our long trip, they were still more infrequent than before. So, when I was asked whether I wanted to take part in a show called *The Club*, I said yes. The program lasted six weeks, and the premise was that three celebrities would be left to look after a bar, along with everything that involved. I would appear on more reality shows going forward—*I'm a Celebrity Get Me Out of Here*, for example—but the one I remember best is still *Celebrity Wife Swap*, which both Myra and I took part in. The program involved two couples swapping partners for one week, and it meant I had to move in with the comedian Freddie Starr, while Myra lived with his wife. It's probably fair to say that Myra won the jackpot there.

I knew of Freddie through Mum, whose friend Terri Christopher had worked with him in the past. Terri was working as a beautician at the time, but in the evenings she would perform at cabaret clubs, occasionally appearing alongside people like Freddie. I remember she would come over to our house sometimes and say things like, "He's a bloody nightmare!" And that was completely understandable. One night, as she was waiting for the curtain to go up ahead of her performance, Freddie came running over and bit her on the bum as hard as he could. He ran off just as the curtain rose, leaving Terri standing there with tears in her eyes from the pain. She had to stop working with him in the end. The man clearly had a screw loose.

Anyway, on *Celebrity Wife Swap*, you didn't find out the identity of the couple you would be swapping with in advance, so when I arrived at the house and spotted a photo of Freddie in the hallway, I immediately froze and took a deep breath. I had assumed they would pair us up with a gay couple, and I really panicked when I realized who I would be spending the week with. As it happens, my worries were quickly justified. Freddie turned out to be a complete control freak, and he refused to let the production team into his house at the times they'd agreed.

His wife, Donna, on the other hand, had a great week with Myra, who also enjoyed her company.

Donna had two children from a previous relationship, and I took the kids on day trips (to a castle, for example). We had a lot of fun together, and when we got home, I cooked them dinner. Freddie and Donna's baby, however, missed her mother, and it pained me to get up in the middle of the night, without Freddie noticing. I would bring her into bed with me. It was, without doubt, the longest week of my life, not just because it was such a pain to be living in the same house as Freddie, but also because I'd never been away from Myra for so long.

Ever since I became famous, I've had stalkers. It began way back in my page three days. I mean, there were people, often teenagers, who wrote to me every single day and who came to all my PAs. When *Touch Me* came out, there was an American boy who sold everything he owned and flew to England to rent a room in a hostel around the corner from my house in Mount Pleasant Villas. He followed me constantly. I knew that because he wrote to me on a daily basis, telling me where I'd been and what I'd been wearing. Dad took the letters to the police, but they said they couldn't do anything because he hadn't broken any laws.

Then there was the man who came over from France. This was after Mum and Dad had separated, which meant I was no longer living at Mount Pleasant Villas. Vanessa, on the other hand, was, and since this bloke never saw me there, he was convinced that Mum and Dad were keeping me prisoner in the basement. He said all this to Vanessa, who told him to shut his mouth. The next day, he jumped out of the bushes and gave her such a fright that she hit him. Another day, he rang the bell, and when Dad and Vanessa came out, he shouted that unless I showed my face immediately, he would kill himself. I was no longer living there, as I've said, and when Dad pointed that out to him yet again, he cut his wrists with a knife, spraying blood everywhere. Dad panicked and called an ambulance, and they never saw him again after that.

Another madman turned up while I was living with Chrissie in Lancaster Gardens. She was working late in the studio one night while I was away, when a bottle of wine came flying in through the window. Chrissie rushed outside and saw a man running down the street. She recognized him—it was the same young man who had already knocked on the door several times that week, sprinting away afterwards. The police managed to work out who he was, but again, they were powerless to do anything. No one had seen him throw the bottle, and so long as he posed no actual physical threat to us, their hands were tied.

Still, these blokes were nothing compared to the man who started creeping around outside the house that Myra and I shared. One day, while I was at the gym, Myra heard someone rattling the lid of our bin. When she looked out of the window, she saw a homeless-looking man with long, straggly hair going through our rubbish bins. She called me to ask what she should do. "Call the police!" I told her, and just as I said it, she saw the man pull on a pair of long, black rubber gloves and walk towards the side entrance. I rushed out of the gym and drove straight home. I knew that the man must have put on the gloves to break one of the windows, but thankfully the police managed to get there and arrest him before anything happened.

Myra later told me that it was the same man who had been writing me letters for two years, threatening to kill her so that he could be with me, attaching pictures of shot and blown-up foxes. She hadn't let me see any of the letters because she didn't want me to worry, but there was a whole stack of them. The police managed to work out that he'd come from a psychiatric hospital in France, where he'd been let out on day release. They sent him straight back, escorted by an English police officer.

In around 2010, the eighties were back in fashion big time, and my telephone started ringing almost nonstop. Suddenly, I found myself being booked for TV shows and gigs all over the world. I did everything, from one-off gigs to huge nostalgia tours with artists like Kim Wilde, Billy Ocean, Bonnie Tyler, Modern Talking, and Shakin' Stevens.

Sabrina was booked to appear in one of those tours, and one day, after a gig, she came over to me and said, "Samantha, we must be friends. We're adults now. We were so big in the eighties, and whenever I perform, your name always comes up—and I think that when you perform, my name comes up."

I nodded gently and tried to work out what she wanted. We'd never really talked properly, after all.

"Samantha . . . I think we should try to put all the bullshit behind us and do a song together."

I just stared at her, and then said, "Really?"

She continued, "Could you write us a song?"

"Uh . . . sure, definitely."

If I'm completely honest, I thought that it sounded like a good idea, especially for the press attention it would generate; and fans we both shared would love it. I was thinking record sales. We swapped email addresses and phone numbers and, after a week or so, spoke on the phone. This time, Sabrina suggested that we do a cover version instead, so that we wouldn't lose any more time. I agreed, and asked which artists she liked.

"Prince."

I liked Prince, too, but Jive had already allowed Tom Jones to do a great cover of "Kiss," and so I suggested something by Debbie Harry instead—she was one of my great idols, after all. "Atomic" was my first thought, followed by "Call Me."

Sabrina thought the latter sounded great and so, not long after that, I recorded my part of the song. I sent the files over to her in Italy so that she could do the same.

The track ended up being a hit in many different countries, and Sabrina and I did a number of gigs together—among them St. Petersburg, which was broadcast to between thirty and forty million viewers.

Suddenly, it felt like all of the pieces had fallen into place again. Not just with regards to my career, but my entire life.

27

FUCK CANCER

It felt like the entire room had started to spin,
and after I put down the phone, I had to take
a deep breath before I could speak to Mum:
"We have to go home."

It all started when Myra began to complain of a toothache. Whenever she ate, I could see just how much pain she was in. Her face twisted, and she would try to chew with her canines on the other side of her mouth.

"You can't go on like this," I said as we sat at the dinner table. "You need to go and see a dentist."

Myra just stared at me. It was no secret that she was terrified of dentists and all medical professionals—I guess because her dad had suffered with cancer for twenty-five years and she had seen a lot of pain as a little girl. She hadn't even wanted to go to the doctor when she went through menopause; it took her six months to finally go and get the tablets she needed. But she was now in so much pain that she didn't know what to do, and so she eventually agreed to see a dentist, who sent her for an x-ray. They established almost immediately that her jaw was broken, and a surgeon took some bone samples to be sent off for analysis.

The results were due the next day, and I went with Myra to the hospital. The minute I saw the doctor, I knew it was bad news.

"Myra, you have angiosarcoma, a very rare form of cancer."

I can only guess how Myra must have felt in that moment. But for me, it was as though the floor had vanished from beneath my feet, and I was in free fall. Yes, I'd suspected that the doctor was bringing bad news, but not that bad. The type of cancer Myra had wasn't just incurable; it was also so uncommon that there was only one doctor in the whole of the UK who specialized in it, and he worked for the British National Health Service (NHS)—which did not have a great reputation at the time. Those working within the national health service were on their knees, and the papers were always full of terrifying reports of a crisis in the nation's hospitals.

Naturally, Myra was worried that she wouldn't get the treatment she needed, but it turned out that the NHS staff were fantastic. And the specialist doctor was also very good. Sadly, he couldn't tell us how long Myra had left—whether it was six months, a year, or longer. At times, that uncertainty was at least as devastating as the fact that Myra was going to die. During the last year we got a private doctor who had saved a baby with a brain tumor, so this was her only chance. Still, we did everything we could to make the most of our time together, and, not long after the diagnosis, I told Myra that she should write a bucket list. I wanted to give her the best possible quality of life during however much time she had left. If she wanted to go on holiday somewhere where the hotels cost eighteen thousand quid a week, or she wanted a private villa, I made sure we did it. And if she wanted to fly in a friend from Scotland or Australia, I made it happen and paid for it, too. All in all, it meant I had to work more than I really wanted to or could cope with.

I remember one particular gig in Stockholm in early 2015. I was due to sing "Touch Me" at the QX Gala there. Myra really wasn't doing well at the time, and I'd barely slept a wink the night before. Back when she was first diagnosed, we continued to sleep together in the same bed, but the treatment she was being given meant that she sweated an incredible amount, and I had recently started sleeping in the room next door, instead. I told her, "That way, you can at least move over to my side of the bed if yours is all sweaty." But she didn't like that, because she thought it meant I didn't want to be with her. In truth, all I wanted was for her to be as comfortable as possible, and though I was in the room next door, I would still go in to see her several times every night.

It meant I was completely exhausted when I arrived in Stockholm, and after checking into the hotel and going up to my room, I fell asleep almost immediately.

My next memory is of my tour manager knocking on my door and saying, "We need to go now."

It turned out Howard had been trying to get hold of me for some time, but that he'd been unable to wake me. I was the secret guest at that evening's gala, and was meant to be closing the entire show.

An hour or so later, I found myself in a dressing room. It was small, with just one window, and I could hear the makeup artists, stylists, and studio hosts shouting to one another in a language I didn't understand on the other side of the door.

The air was close and difficult to breathe. Given the chance, I would have left. Given the chance, I would have been by Myra's side. The uncertainty . . . Not having any idea how long she had left. Not having any idea whether she would be alive when I woke up. Everything felt like it was a haze.

Someone knocked on the door. Shouted through the crack, "Five minutes."

I hauled myself up, pulled on my leather jacket. Paused in front of the mirror.

From the stage, I could hear the intro to the song that had brought me there. Next thing I knew, someone had handed me a microphone and I had made my way out into the bright spotlights on shaking legs.

Myra gradually got worse and worse, and the doctors eventually told us that the chemotherapy was no longer working. They said all they could do was attempt to prolong her life with medication.

She was taking morphine for the pain, which got worse and worse as time went on, eventually making it impossible for me to leave her. All I really wanted to do was take care of her, as I was her carer. I was losing the person I had loved for seventeen years. I had no choice but to leave, at least a few times a month, because I needed to pay our bills.

Ahead of one trip with work, I called Myra's friend Kay, who lived in Australia, and asked whether she would come to stay while I flew to Israel to film an ad. It was good money, so I only had to work once that month. I paid for Kay's flight and felt a strange mix of gratitude towards Kay and anxiety for Myra when, on the day I was due to leave, I got into the taxi after kissing Myra goodbye. As usual we cuddled for ages as if I would never see her again, but I had to work to pay for the private health care to prolong her life.

Mum came with me to Tel Aviv, and as I rehearsed with the male actor I would be appearing alongside on the second day, she came in and said that she'd just found out that Cilla Black had died. I was upset, because Cilla Black had always been a great idol of mine, and I'd also met her on a few occasions. Taking direction there by the swimming pool wasn't all that easy after hearing the news.

That evening, Mum and I were rehearsing a scene in the living room of our suite when the phone rang. I picked up, and knew immediately from Kay's voice that something was wrong.

"Myra had a cardiac arrest; she's been taken to hospital. It was a small one, and they managed to get her heart going again in the ambulance, but it's still serious."

It felt like the entire room had started to spin, and after I put down the phone, I had to take a deep breath before I could speak to Mum: "We have to go home."

We went straight into the bedroom, dragged our suitcases onto the double bed, and began to pack. It was like everything to do with the film shoot had vanished from my mind. The fact it was a big production with over a hundred extras, and the fact I would be losing out on fifty thousand pounds, obviously meant nothing at all in that moment.

As I stood there, folding clothes into my suitcase, I noticed an all-too-familiar scent. Myra used to wear an exclusive perfume called Molecule, and that was the fragrance that was currently filling my nose. I glanced around, my heart pounding in my chest. Since Tel Aviv was so hot, the windows were closed and the air conditioning was on. That meant the scent could hardly be coming from anywhere outside the room. It also didn't seem likely that it was coming from any of my clothes, since they were all freshly washed.

I went out into the living room to get Mum, who had gone to make sure she hadn't forgotten anything. When we went back into the bedroom, the smell of the perfume was as clear as before, and I heard Mum gasp, "My God, you're right, that's Myra's perfume!"

At that very moment, the phone rang. It was Kay, calling to say that Myra had just passed away peacefully, not long after she arrived at the hospital. I couldn't get my breath through crying. I felt helpless and so far away. The journey home took an eternity. I couldn't even speak. All I did was snuggle up to Mum and cry all the way home.

Over the days that followed, a lot of the newspapers got in touch to offer huge sums of money for the rights to publish the pictures of Myra's funeral. I'd always thought it was sick that they did that kind of thing—and that certain celebrities agreed to it—but at that particular moment in time, it actually felt more offensive.

To stop the paparazzi and everyone else from disrupting the ceremony, we had to change churches several times. The entire service was very private, with only Myra's closest friends and relatives in attendance, and we released white doves into the air once it was over.

That was when the next strange thing happened: my dove refused to fly away. I tried to make it leave my cupped hands, to help it swing up into the air with gentle wing strokes. It was only after what felt like an eternity that it spread its wings and flew away over the leafy treetops surrounding the cemetery. The woman who'd brought the doves said this had never happened before in her twenty-five years of working with doves.

I didn't dare say anything at the time, but I had an almost overwhelming feeling that it was Myra, not wanting to leave me alone.

That Christmas, Mum and I traveled to the island in Thailand that Myra and I had returned to many times since my year out, and after just a few days there, my senses started to return. It was as though the sunlight didn't just fill the air; it had also started to work its way inside me.

Sadly, on one of our first evenings there, Mum managed to trip on the stairs up to the loft where she slept. She landed so badly that she managed to damage a couple of ribs, meaning she had to fly home a few days later. She told me I needed to stay, as I had to lay Myra to rest where she wanted to be.

I stayed behind, and one evening, the time finally came for something I'd made up my mind to do the minute we booked the trip. Myra had loved the island so much, after all, and it felt only right that it should be her final resting place.

I'd brought her ashes with me, and I asked my friend Jon, who had originally told us about the island and who was staying in his house there at the time, to come with me. So, with the urn in my arms, Jon and I took to the water in one of the local fishermen's boats. There wasn't a breath of air, and the sun had started to glow increasingly red on the horizon.

As the outboard motor stopped and the silence enveloped us, I took the lid off the urn and emptied Myra's ashes into the sea. Though I felt a kind of serene satisfaction at having been able to fulfill what I knew was Myra's last wish, I was obviously also weighed down by so much sorrow that I couldn't bring myself to say any goodbyes. Instead, Jon said a few deep, beautiful words as the water lapped quietly at the sides of our boat, and a seabird cried out high above us.

28

NEXT YEAR

"Happy birthday to you, happy birthday to you, happy birthday, dear Sammy, happy birthday to you!"

The words, sung by more than a hundred people, rise up towards the treetops in my garden on this beautiful April evening, and I shiver—not so much from the hint of chill that has crept in as dusk approaches, but from the wonderful warmth of all of my relatives and friends.

I hadn't planned to celebrate my fiftieth birthday at all. But at the same time, I know that this is the start of a new chapter in my life. And that's why I've gathered all of my nearest and dearest here, around me.

My friend Peter, a music producer, cautiously starts up the music. He's promised to be DJ for the evening. Mum's closest neighbor is looking after the food. She's from Pakistan, so the scents drifting across the garden are fantastic.

I'm given a couple of congratulations and kisses on the cheek, and glance over to Linda, who is talking to Mum. We've met as friends a number times over the last few years, but now we've taken the next step, and I'm deeply grateful that I've been given the chance to love again.

I can see that Linda is nervous, and I understand that. I'm nervous, too. I mean, many of the people here are meeting her for the first time today.

But I soon see her relax. Everyone shows that they like her.

I smile, and am suddenly struck by the thought that, given everything I've gone through over the past few years, I should be bitter. But, as I raise my champagne glass to Linda and she smiles back, all I feel is a wave of gratitude washing over me.

ACKNOWLEDGMENTS

SAMANTHA FOX:

First of all, I would like to thank my beautiful Mummy, Carole. Without her by my side, my career would never have happened! Love you so much, xx.

Thank you to my solid friends who have always been there for me: Colin, Julie, Dawn, Celeste, Tee, Saffron, Pauline, my friend and partner at Fox 2000, Howard Marshall, my mate Pete Martine for the home cooked meals and fab remixes, my financial advisor, Chris Turner, my agent, Kevin Moss, Kay Goddard, Craig and Emma at Unleashed PR, and Joel for the website.

My amazing band, Jonny, Ross, Andy, Tee and Jem, my dancers, Dani, Rachel, Bexi, Kathryn and Laura, my producers, Ian Masterson (can't wait for the new album) and Jon Moon, Dr. Jason Fletcher for artwork, and Martin and Leif for the help with writing this book.

A big thank you to my Foxy Fans who have always supported and believed in me and kept me going, especially Dimitris, Oren, Fabien, and Franck.

I'm really looking forward to my future with my Linda and her wonderful sons.

All my love,
Sammy
xx

THE CO-AUTHORS, LEIF ERIKSSON AND MARTIN SVENSSON:

Sam Fox, Myra Stratton, Howard Marshall, Carole Fox, Colin Bryan, Celeste Bivetto, Oren Ovadia, Dimitris Voulgaris, Jon Astrop, Linda Olsen, and the Olsen boys. Last but not least, we would like to thank Alice Menzies, our publishers around the globe, and our great agents at www.arenascripts.com.

INDEX